Caught Off Guard:

A Testimony of Overcoming Suffering Through
Trusting God and Embracing Community

ASHLEY BACHMANN

Caught Off Guard: A Testimony of Overcoming Suffering Through Trusting God and Embracing Community

Trilogy Christian Publishers A Wholly Owned Subsidiary of Trinity Broadcasting Network

2442 Michelle Drive Tustin, CA 92780

Rights Department, 2442 Michelle Drive, Tustin, CA 92780.
Trilogy Christian Publishing/TBN and colophon are trademarks of Trinity Broadcasting Network.

Cover design by: Kristy Swank

For information about special discounts for bulk purchases, please contact Trilogy Christian Publishing.
Trilogy Disclaimer: The views and content expressed in this book are those of the author and may not necessarily reflect the views and doctrine of Trilogy Christian Publishing or the Trinity Broadcasting Network.

In order to protect the privacy of individuals, some names and details have been changed in this book.

10 9 8 7 6 5 4 3 2 1
Library of Congress Cataloging-in-Publication Data is available.
ISBN: 979-8-89041-493-9
E-ISBN: 979-8-89041-494-6

TABLE OF CONTENTS

Foreword

My privilege has been to read a lot of books through the years. I seriously began reading in Bible college and soon learned what a blessing it is to actually enjoy it.

Here was where I began to study and not just passively read the words.

Then, I had to learn how to read, not to study but to simply understand. I became fascinated with so many different kinds of books and authors. Fiction, nonfiction, humor, serious, mystery, etc.

Recently, I was introduced to a book written by Ashley as a rough draft, and I found it was such a powerful word of testimony I encouraged her to finish it.

I have known Ashley for a number of years, and I have appreciated her heart and sincerity. She writes with a passion to reveal her real personal trials and testimony. This is not a fictional book. As you read it, I believe it will encourage you in your trials and situations as well.

With this book comes a promise from the Word of God, which says, "No temptation has overtaken you except such as is common to man; but God is faithful, who will not allow you to be tempted beyond what you are able, but with the temptation will also make the way of escape, that you may be able to bear it" (1 Corinthians 10:13, NKJV).

Read this book with faith in your heart and believe as she has written, knowing that all things work together for our good (Romans 8:28), not only in her life but in yours as well as a believer.

Dr. Terry Brown, DMIN

*And they overcame him by the blood of the
Lamb and by the word of their testimony.*

Revelation 12:11 (NKJV)

This verse crossed my path a few times as I walked through a dark valley. It triggered a different outlook each time I saw it. The verse reminded me that suffering is temporary. I knew when my battle ended, there would be a testimony.

As you read my story, I hope you grow in how loving God is. He was ever present in my life during the good, bad, and ugly. Others may have perceived or recalled different details, but these are my recollections. My story fluctuates from moments of pure joy to traumatic events. As well as suffering to a degree I didn't know existed. I am sure others have experienced circumstances much worse while others less. Today, I understand suffering much differently, and my heart aches for the suffering.

I relate suffering to physical pain. As a registered nurse, I learned through experience that a patient's pain is what a patient says it is. For instance, a back injury may cause mild pain for one patient and severe for another. Pain tolerance may be attributed to many things. However, pain is what a patient says it is. You can't change it. Suffering is the same, and my suffering in this story was the worst I've ever known. Somehow, I kept in mind it could always get worse. I experienced my all-time low, and by God's grace, I survived. The wounds were deep and infected at times, but through God's power and love, I am healed. Where wounds once existed, I now bear scars. I discovered a deeper level of God's goodness throughout the suffering. During my battle, the Holy Spirit provided an interesting perspective of the following verse. It transformed me and how I respond and see others.

*Some men came, bringing to him a paralyzed man, carried by four of
them. Since they could not get him to Jesus because of the crowd, they made
an opening in the roof above Jesus by digging through it and then lowered
the mat the man was lying on. When Jesus saw their faith, he said to the
paralyzed man, "Son, your sins are forgiven."*

Mark 2:3–5 (NIV)

Caught Off Guard

Chapter 1

———⚮———

King of the Mountain

I begin with my healing testimony; it taught me a valuable lesson in word choice. The lesson, unbeknownst to me, prepared me for the future. In just a few years, a series of unexpected catastrophic events would enter my timeline. A firm foundation and spiritual warfare weapons were developed in my healing process. Spiritual warfare weapons were added to my arsenal. I was fortunate to be in my late thirties before I experienced my first bout of suffering as I faced the unknown.

It was mid-morning, the day after Halloween, and life was going as planned. I was at the office and worked diligently to complete my daily checklist. I suddenly felt my heart start racing, and I was confused because I was at rest. Shortly after, I felt lightheaded and had been close to having a syncopal (faint) episode. I sat up straight and took a few deep breaths, hoping it would vanish. I realized I had not eaten and believed my blood sugar was low. I ate a snack, drank some water, and refilled my coffee cup. I began working on my checklist, and the symptoms subsided.

A little while later, the symptoms returned with a little more intensity. Now, there was discomfort in my chest, and I began to feel hot and sweaty. I hadn't ever felt this type of discomfort and became scared when it didn't go away. My mind ran through possible causes, and the feeling of passing out intensified. I worried about losing consciousness because I felt it was coming. My boss was concerned as she noticed I was in distress; she took me to a local clinic for an evaluation. I was advised to seek further evaluation at a local emergency room and went directly to the hospital. After hours of evaluation and testing, the physician said I could go home. The clinic and hospital relayed I had an abnormal EKG (electrocardiogram). I received instructions to follow up with a cardiologist. I felt better and had not experienced an episode since being at the clinic. I was eager to get home and began the one-hour drive.

I was on a dark two-lane highway and neared the halfway point. Suddenly, without notice, my heart began to race. I could feel the heartbeats pounding in my chest. Along came shortness of breath, profuse sweating, and a terrifying feeling like my life was leaving my body. I pulled over onto the shoulder, fearing I was going to lose consciousness. I tried relief measures, and nothing helped. I could not think of anything else to do and dialed 911.

First Responders arrived on the scene quickly. I was never so happy to see a human face. I was stabilized and secured in the ambulance, then transported to a local hospital. I was evaluated by another emergency room physician and received orders to follow up with a cardiologist. Confusion and worry set in on the way home; I received no diagnosis or explanation of what happened. This episode (near death, to me), coupled with no explanations, created an overwhelming fear of dying. I knew something was terribly wrong with me. It was not normal to be in that type of distress. The unknowns set into motion a constant cycle of negative thoughts and worries. The fear of dying in the car was so paralyzing I didn't drive for a month. I worked from home and relied on people to help me run errands and grocery shop.

I saw my primary physician and a local cardiologist. Both physicians performed evaluations and testing. Neither seemed to find anything significant. The cardiologist referred me to a cardiac electrophysiologist who began a series of tests. The testing period was slow and took months. It was difficult knowing it would be a while before I got answers. The first test was a Holter monitor. It was ordered for ninety continuous days. I wore the monitor twenty-four hours a day except when showering. Every time an episode hit me, I had to press a button. The button marked each episode. The marks made it easier for the interpreter assigned to read the recording. My primary physician had already ordered a Holter monitor, but it was only for seventy-two hours. I was not optimistic because they did not find anything significant. However, if only mild episodes were captured in the seventy-two hours, in ninety days, they should be able to capture more.

During the ninety days, I felt anxious as episodes came and went. I felt they didn't care how distressing the episodes were. I wished I could have explained how awful it felt. Many years later, this illustration came to mind and put it in a unique perspective. I think it would have helped the medical team understand. It depicted what I felt during an episode.

It is a comparison of two drivers of a manual transmission vehicle. The experience with each driver was distinctly different. Both experiences were in fast muscle cars with stick shifts. The good driver accelerated quickly and shifted through the gears smoothly. The good driver handled the car with finesse, and the ride was smooth. The bad driver had difficulty shifting when he accelerated to high speeds. I heard the car disagreeing when the RPMs topped out, and there was no correction. The engine was revving up in a roar like it was warning the driver to adjust. The bad driver seemed confused and shifted to the wrong gear. The car jerked, popped, and felt like it hit an imaginary wall of resistance. Then, I heard the vehicle quiet down like it was losing power or going to die. The car slowed down softly, roaring as it tried to acclimate to the wrong gear. Eventually, it adjusted and was back to normal.

My normal, healthy heart was like the ride with the good driver. However, my episodes were like the ride with the bad driver. My heart rate took off, racing and topping out, and I did not feel discomfort in this phase. As my body attempted to adjust and find the right gear, the discomfort ensued. Once my body chose a different gear (hitting the wall of resistance), that is when the most uncomfortable symptoms manifested. Finally, like the car sounding like it was losing power or going to die, I also felt this in my body. Eventually, my body acclimated to the internal adjustments, and I returned to normal.

Fear grew at a high rate of speed as the episodes persisted, and I knew it would be months before I had an answer. It caused me to become physically sicker, taking a toll on my gastrointestinal system. My appetite vanished, and I lost weight. My muscle mass began to atrophy, and I looked anorexic. Along with the cardiac symptoms, I became short of breath with minimal exertion. My health was worse than that of the elderly patients I took care of in my nursing field. I could only walk within the house, or I would have an episode. I walked to the mailbox one day while I was on the phone and had to hang up because I was so short of breath. I placed myself into a pit of darkness, focusing on the fear of the unknown. In the pit, I continually ran through the worst-case scenarios. I thought I was being cautious and a realist from a medical scientific perspective. Subsequently, I was hurting myself with every word, thought, and action that contradicted God's word.

The last test the cardiac electrophysiologist ordered was a tilt test. It shows how various positions affect your heart rate, heart rhythm, and blood pressure. Information from the tilt test can help determine the causes of lightheadedness, dizziness, and fainting spells (syncope). The tilt test was quite an experience, and I laugh about it now, but it was no laughing matter then.

The technician began by strapping me to a table in a supine position. Sticky electrodes were placed on my chest wall, a blood pressure cuff secured on my arm, and a pulse oximeter on my finger. The table slowly tilted upwards in timed increments. I experienced no problems during the tilting phase, fifteen to twenty minutes. The table had tilted all the way up to a standing position. I thought the test was complete and asked how I did. I also felt what a wasted trip. The technician said the test was not over. He administered a medication, inducing a vasovagal response. If you ever have a vasovagal response, you will never forget it.

A vasovagal response is a sudden drop in heart rate and blood pressure, leading to fainting. Vasovagal symptoms include fainting, fatigue, sudden waves of heat (warm feeling), profuse sweating, palpitations, heart rate changes, blurred vision, fear, and nausea.

Within moments of taking the medication, my heart rate increased, and I felt a sudden wave of heat. Soon after, my heart started racing, and my respirations increased with shortness of breath. I was beginning to feel the sensation I experienced in my car. Within a matter of seconds, the symptoms were so intense I felt like death. I asked the technician to please stop. He replied this was the most important part of the test and it would not be too much longer. I barely had the energy to talk or hold my head up. All of a sudden, an intense sensation of having a bowel movement hit me. With the last bit of energy left in me, I had a last request. It was an embarrassing plea to the technician (a Hail Mary, if you will). "Sir, sir, will you stop? I'm about to poop on myself." He replied, "No!" I didn't even have the energy to be upset. I felt like I was dying and accepted it as I lowered my head.

Unexpectantly, the table started lowering back down, and I felt immediate relief. Once I returned to the flat position, the technician unstrapped me and said I could get up, pointing to the restroom. I jumped down from the table and went straight to the potty, only to realize the urge to have a bowel movement no longer existed. I could not believe the strong urge to have a bowel movement occurred so quickly and left just as fast!

During this battle, I was confused and scared about the drastic decline in my health. I became frustrated at the long testing process. I was not getting answers, and I became desperate for help, but not through medicine. I started watching gospel TV shows and reading books. I hoped to learn something from God. I did not know what I was searching for. I caught the end of a TV show and heard a man speaking. It stopped me in my tracks. He was teaching on our imagination.[1] I remember thinking to myself, "What did he say about God's Word?" He delivered God's word so simply but with revelation to a degree which I had not experienced.

I immediately went to his website and checked it out. I scrolled down to audio teachings, and the first one that caught my eye was called "Sharper Than a Two-Edged Sword," and it changed my life. The day I heard this lesson, I took a dramatic turn in my life. This was the beginning of my discovery of the power of God's word and promises. The more I listened, the more I craved to learn more about God's word. It was not an immediate fix, but as I learned more, I became stronger each day. I wrote down healing and encouraging scriptures in a notebook. I declared the promises in the Scriptures often, and every time I felt an episode. I felt myself being built up the more I believed and declared. The frequency of the cardiac symptoms grew longer apart, finally dissipating and never returning.

---

1   *The Power of Imagination*, Andrew Wommack.

King of the Mountain

I learned God's word had to be a planted seed to see a harvest. Andrew Wommack provided a simple yet powerful illustration. The illustration was with a coffee cup in his message "You've Already Got It." I am paraphrasing Mr. Wommack's teaching of Isaiah 53:5 when he says, "By His stripes, you are healed," with emphasis on *are*. In his teaching, I understood healing is available to us by the stripes Jesus bore. Thank goodness, it was not written that healing is available by good works, church attendance, or honorable deeds. You see, there is no criteria or work you or I can do to receive healing. Healing is a gift from God. In Andrew Wommack's teaching, he said to use this coffee cup and pretend it's healing. He says, "Here is your cup of coffee," and hands it to you. Andrew went on to say, "Now what if someone comes along and says, 'Give that cup back'?" Andrew asked, "Will you release it or hold onto it?" Obviously, I would hold onto it and dare someone to take it from me. Healing is the same way—it is mine.

I created my own healing illustration from that teaching. It was from a game I played in my childhood called King of the Mountain. As a child, when we stumbled upon a large mound of dirt, someone rushed to the top, claiming to be King of the Mountain. It was a challenge to take that person down and become the new king. I grew up with boys and developed a competitive nature because of it. This childhood game was perfect in relation to my new insight of healing. Now, as a grown woman, I imagined I was the King of the Mountain, holding onto my healing. I would do everything I recently learned to remain king. I would continue declaring and standing on God's word.

I learned there are multiple things that could dethrone me from the mountain, such as how people talked to me and my thoughts. Doubt could take root through medical science, such as lab reports, doctor's reports, and physical symptoms. Interestingly, people I loved had the potential to dethrone me. I was careful around all people.

Their conversation contained words of caution or care but were negative at the root. A genuine question asking how I was doing would be enough to cause doubt to enter. I had to continually be on alert when speaking to all people.

I learned how to answer the frequent question, "How are you doing?" I answered with something true, but I added a promise or praise report before ending the sentence. I would respond with, "My day was rough, but each day I do better." I might also say, "I am doing okay today. I am glad I am no longer short of breath." When my mind shifted toward my symptoms, I opposed it a few ways. I spoke a promise from God's word or praised Him and gave thanks.

Initially, the symptoms were so frequent and intense that I continually had to focus on giving thanks and praise. I gave praise for each new day and the things we take for granted, such as breathing on our own, vision, hearing, and use of extremities, just to name a few. I expressed thankfulness when the episodes went from every half hour to every hour, even if the days were rough. I purposed in my heart that no symptom or medical report would cause me to topple off my mountain. I might slip and lose my footing for a moment. However, I was determined I would not come down from my healing mountain. I remained king as I clung to God's promises.

The timing was perfect (learning what God's word said about healing) in demonstrating my faith. I dealt with the heart episodes for approximately four months while seeking answers and a diagnosis. I had an appointment with the cardiac electrophysiologist to review test results, diagnosis, and prognosis. He relayed I had supraventricular tachycardia (SVT), and its causes range from heart disease, chronic lung disease, a lot of caffeine, drug misuse, and other reasons. A typical heart beats about 60 to 100 times a minute. During an episode of SVT, the heart beats about 150 to 220 times a minute and faster or slower. SVT is not usually life-threatening; however, in extreme cases, an episode of SVT may cause unconsciousness or cardiac arrest. I do not remember which type of SVT my cardiologist diagnosed me with. He recommended medications and a surgery option if I did not respond well to the medication. I listened to his report and treatment options. I told myself I would not take the medication or follow the plan. I decided to stand in faith and trust God. By the stripes of Jesus, I walked right out of SVT into healing, and it has not returned. Once it disappeared, I stood on this verse: "Affliction will not rise up a second time" (Nahum 1:9, NKJV).

This battle taught me valuable lessons and placed godly people in my path. Veronica and Crystal taught me how to pray in a small group setting, not the begging kind of prayers. The seed they planted turned out to be a weapon of survival. I discovered the importance of speaking to my symptoms and became familiar with this scripture.

For verily I say unto you, That whosoever shall say unto this mountain, Be thou removed, and be thou cast into the sea; and shall not doubt in his heart, but shall believe that those things which he saith shall come to pass; he shall have whatsoever he saith. Therefore I say unto you, What things soever ye desire, when ye pray, believe that ye receive them, and ye shall have them.

Mark 11:23–24 (KJV)

I realized every word we choose is life or death, and we must choose wisely. I could see how insignificant my current priorities were in life. My eyes opened to the significance of the simple things. I became a more thankful person. My faith grew exponentially. I walked away from this attack on my health with a new understanding of how powerful God's word is.

Your world is being framed by the words of your mouth.

Pastor Duane Sheriff

Sermon series "The Mystery of Seeds"

The Fisherman

The day was sunny with a gentle breeze perfect for fishing. The fisherman often daydreams about these days. The weather, conditions, and the fisherman's schedule just so happened to align. Today, the fisherman's daydream has become reality. The anticipation of the day had been building, and now he started his journey.

The fisherman excitedly headed to his favorite fishing hole. He walked through a pasture into the thick woods. There, he followed a dirt path the animals had trodden down. The fisherman hurriedly walked, trying to reach his fishing spot, ready to enjoy the afternoon. The fisherman envisioned the plans in his mind. He saw relaxation, the catch of the day, ending with a fish fry. Every detail of the day trip was falling into place just like he pictured.

The fisherman was minding his own business and did not have a care in the world. Unexpectedly, he lost his balance on a slight slope, sliding down onto the ground. His hand landed just outside the dirt path into the weeds and tall grass. His hand caught traction from the weeds, stopping a continual slide down the slope. Once the fisherman stopped sliding, he gathered his thoughts and oriented himself. Unbeknownst to the fisherman, a venomous snake lay quietly hidden underneath the tall grass, and it struck his hand. The fisherman discovered he was injured in his rush and slight venture off the path.

Chapter 2

—✼—

The Story Book Beginning

I was thirty-nine when I began working at a brand-new large clinic. I was hired to oversee the clinical aspects of the facility. It was hectic initially until the learning curve flattened. I met many new staff members as I familiarized myself to the specialty areas. A couple of months after the clinic opened, I met Brennan. He was a healthcare professional selling his private practice before he transitioned to the clinic. Brennan's department experienced a delay in opening due to construction. He took pride in his department, and I appreciated his motivation to provide quality patient care. It was a relief to work with managers who took the initiative in their respective departments.

We later discovered we were experiencing similar life challenges. We were experiencing marital problems that eventually ended in divorce. We had been in our first marriages for over twenty years. This opened the door to conversation and understanding for one another.

Brennan is very talkative and a storyteller. I am more of a listener, so our conversations flowed for hours. We began hanging out when we discovered we had common interests. We shared the same energy and enjoyed the same things. We later started dating as our compatibility was perfect, and we got along very well. We loved to golf, travel, and watch movies. Brennan was kind and thoughtful towards me. He continually stayed connected, day and night, via text or calls. I found his intelligence and confidence an attractive quality. Brennan also showed a playful and funny side that I found quite charming. Brennan liked to be the center of my attention, and he made me feel like I was the center of his.

Brennan and I enjoyed each other in fun times and in the simple tasks or chores. We worked well together when he had personal projects. On Tuesdays or Wednesdays, he would text me the plans for the upcoming weekend. He lined out all the activities and meal plans from Friday's end of business to Sunday evening. I had been in charge at work and home for so long, and even though his planning was odd to me, I liked it. Every time I arrived at his house, he was outside, awaiting my arrival. He had the garage door open and closed it as soon as I parked. He opened my car door and greeted me with a warm embrace. He helped me gather my belongings and carried them in. I felt like royalty each time; it never got old.

Not only did he plan our weekend, but he also covered all the costs. I had a tough time getting used to him paying for everything. I felt guilty for the longest time and offered to pay continually. He declined and refused to accept any money. He finally, after several months, allowed me to buy movie tickets. I snuck that in by purchasing ahead online after he told me about the movie we were watching. After we got more serious, Brennan would text a trip suggestion. Once he got my "Yes, I would love to go!" He did all the planning. He planned every detail of our trips and covered all the costs. I felt like I needed to pay for something, but he never asked. He always declined if I offered to pay for anything. He seemed content that I was willing to go. He said he was excited about experiencing the trips together.

Brennan went out of his way to do special things for me. He might buy (in bulk) my favorite candy or surprise me with a nice gift. We held hands constantly, no matter if we watched TV, walked, or rode in the car. Brennan cooked for me, always helped in the kitchen, and made sure I had coffee. The longer we were together, the stronger our bond grew. We began to enjoy each other's company in all areas of life. We became all we needed as we partnered up in both fun and work. When we were together, it felt like the world stopped, and it was just the two of us. We had our own sphere of existence and needed nothing else.

One day, we were lying on the couch watching TV. I do not have the words to properly explain what happened. The only words that come to mind are "an extraordinary feeling." We were both facing the TV and began a conversation. I sat up and shifted to face him. In perfect sync, we stopped talking. We gazed into one another's eyes as the sound of the TV diminished. Strangely, the conversation ceased, yet it felt like something of great magnitude was accomplished. Moments later, in perfect sync, we started talking again as if nothing happened.

On my way home that evening, Brennan called. He brought up the couch incident and what he felt. It was an overwhelming feeling of love and acceptance for one another. Neither one of us knew how to describe it and agreed it was profound.

There was one quality in Brennan that outshined them all. Brennan said he was a Christian. He went to a local non-denominational church with regular attendance. I was ecstatic because I was non-denominational and attended church regularly. He told me about his mission trip to Haiti with his daughter. I was a fan based on those details alone. He said he gave a motorcycle to the church. His donation was a generous act, and I felt he must love God and His people. Brennan said he attended a small men's group, and I was glad to hear that because I feel it's a deeper connection to the church body.

Two years later, Brennan proposed, and my answer was yes without hesitation. Brennan continually shared his feelings about how special I was to him. I felt important to him, and we belonged together forever. Brennan shared these texts, which provided insight into how much I meant to him. My fiancé wrote:

"You are a blessing to your fiancé. When we met, I wasn't looking for my soulmate. I was a man that was confused and needed a friend, someone to distract me from all the bad. The person I found was incredible; she was warm and caring. She made me a better person and continues to do that every day. So yes, you are the woman I prayed for. I love you more each day. Now, I get to share and spend my life with her. That's amazing!

"... I love doing anything with you. You make my life better.

"It's strange how strongly connected I am to you. I've never felt this way about anyone before. It's a great feeling to have.

"I haven't felt love in a long, long time. You have warmed my heart.

"Nothing feels right unless you're by my side.

"I enjoy spending time with you. I do things with you that I never did with my X. That makes our relationship very special to me."

Brennan asked me what my top three wedding destinations were. Hawaii was the most preferred, and we agreed upon it. Brennan spared no expense in booking our trips, especially this one. I reached out and covered the wedding planner after he gave me the itinerary.

We set the day for early July. We were going to Kauai Island first, then Maui. We planned four days in Kauai, ending with our elopement ceremony before going to Maui. The first day was a struggle as we fought jet lag and the five-hour time change. Once we landed and got into our vehicle, I became preoccupied with sightseeing. Kauai Island and the town we landed in was small. It was like being in rural Oklahoma, except it was a tropical island. Travel through the town was effortless, with no major highways or backups. Once we drove out of the small town, it was open fields and mountains in the distance. Tropical trees and plants aligned the roadsides and covered the land. There were specific trees that stood out all over the island. The trees were tall and grew in groups. The branches of the trees overlapped with one another and formed natural canopies. I can spot these trees in movies now! A strange sighting was the site of all the free-roaming chickens on the island. The chickens were in town and country and on a golf course. Momma chicks and her baby chicks marched up and down the roadways. It's like they owned the place. No one bothered or paid them attention.

We had reservations at the Grand Hyatt Resort, approximately thirty minutes from the airport. It is a beautiful resort in a remote area located on the ocean. We were greeted with fresh leis upon arrival, and the flowers were flawless. We checked in at the registration desk and made our way to the room. Our room was oceanfront with spectacular views of the resort and beach. Once our luggage arrived at our room, we changed into our swimsuits.

We walked around exploring the resort and pool area. The weather was perfect, and I couldn't wait to get into the ocean water. I heard the waves calling from the pool area. We both were ready to jump into the ocean and headed to the swim area. A man met us on his way out and cautioned us, saying the waves were strong. I looked at Brennan, and we gave him the "Yeah, right" look. We entered the ocean and began wading out to deeper water.

Before long, I realized the waves were stronger than the ones I was used to in Florida. I was greeted with a strong Hawaiian wave, and it slammed me down onto the ocean floor. The wave knocked my bathing suit out of sorts, and I lost my sunglasses. I struggled briefly to get myself together, and Brennan retrieved my sunglasses. Afterward, we laughed about it, and I was glad that the man didn't witness it.

We enjoyed our first few days on the island with activities and sightseeing. We took a helicopter ride to see the entire layout of the island, including areas where a scene from Jurassic Park was filmed. The majority of the island is inhabitable and mountainous. We drove around one day, and it only took thirty to forty minutes to get to the other side of the island. We golfed one day, and it was an amazing course with natural beauty, ocean views, and crowing chickens.

We married on a Monday, and it was a private ceremony on Pu'u Poa Beach near Princeville Resort. We had a sunset ceremony, so we had the day to prepare. Brennan and I enjoyed the first part of the day together. I planned a hair and makeup session in my room after lunch. Brennan left the room during our session. The hair and makeup lady arrived with my fresh tropical hairpiece that matched the bouquet. She had a picture of the hairstyle I wanted and began her magic. She did a cut crease eye makeup look. I was not crazy about it until I saw how nice it looked in the photos. Once she finished, I called Brennan back to the room, and we finished getting ready.

We had a twenty-to-thirty-minute drive to Princeville Resort. Upon arrival, the lighting and timing could not have been more perfect. It was sunny with scattered rain clouds as the sun was going to set within the next hour. The sun cast a burnt orange color while the clouds had a bluish-grey hue in the sky. A little rain fell during the photo session. In the photos, the rain looked like glitter. The wedding planner brought my bouquet and his and her leis for the ceremony. The orchids in my pieces were white with a bold violet color. The flower shop did an amazing job and recreated the exact idea I had sent months before.

The preacher surprised us during the middle of the ceremony when he asked us to share wedding vows with one another. I scrambled around momentarily, trying to decide what I was going to say. Brennan vowed to love and care for me. I vowed to Brennan that I would show him God's kind of love (to my limited understanding) for the rest of his life. My vow moved me because I knew it was a special love, and it brought tears to my eyes. God's kind of love is not common, and it touches you deeply when you experience it. The ceremony was everything I imagined it would be and more. At the conclusion of our ceremony, we had our first dinner as husband and wife at the Princeville Resort.

The next morning, we set out for Maui for our honeymoon. Brennan booked the remaining days at the Ritz Carlton, and I was awestruck. I had never stayed at a Ritz Carlton, and it was breathtaking. The resort had large exotic flower arrangements everywhere. The arrangements contained multiple floral varieties with bold, vivid colors, and they had a waxy appearance. I found myself touching every arrangement to check the authenticity. Upon arrival at the Ritz Carlton Resort, we received the Aloha greeting along with fresh leis. When we entered our suite, there was champagne and fresh flowers with congratulations. The suite was spacious with a living area, kitchen, and separate bedroom and bathroom. We enjoyed exploring the island of Maui for the rest of our stay. We drove the road to Hana and experienced snorkeling adventures, golf at Kapalua Plantation course, and a scary car ride up to the Haleakala Volcano. I enjoyed snorkeling the most because the coral reef and sea life were out of this world. Sea turtles swam up to me as though they were greeting me. I had never seen that kind of sea life or structures on the ocean floor. It seemed like time flew, and before long, it was time to return. I was excited about returning as husband and wife and living together under one roof.

Brennan stopped working at the clinic and officially retired from his medical profession before we married. Shortly after Oklahoma approved medical marijuana, Brennan and his best friend (BFF) of twenty years were on a new venture. Brennan and BFF were planning on growing marijuana. While we dated, Brennan saw a promising future with me. He asked my thoughts before he jumped into the marijuana business. I told Brennan it did not bother me, and I supported his new pursuit. Brennan and BFF were 50/50 partners in the new business and soon became busy with the marijuana grow construction. They hired a man from Colorado to head the grow operations. The year after we married, the company was busy as production and business demands pressed in. Brennan and BFF were also in the works of starting a marijuana drink business. Brennan and BFF needed manpower and financial support to reach their marijuana business goals. They added three new business partners to the marijuana grow, Texan and the Twins. Brennan, Texan, and the Twins were to focus on the grow. BFF would focus on the drink business. Brennan asked me multiple times to quit my job and help him. He was working long hours, requiring extensive manual labor, almost seven days a week. Brennan expressed how much help and support I could provide in all his businesses. He also pitched the idea of having flexibility in my schedule and being available to my son. He finally convinced me things would be okay and that he would take care of me no matter what. Eleven months after we married, I resigned from my position and joined Brennan. I hit the ground running from day one. We worked well together and accomplished a lot as a team. Neither one of us had experience with the marijuana plant, and it was all new. The manual labor involved was highly underestimated. I have never worked so hard in my life.

Chapter 3

———— ∞ ————

The Day My Life Changed

You intended to harm me, but God intended it all for good.

Genesis 50:20 (NLT)

It was an extremely cold February day. I was glad I was working at home. Brennan asked me to work on bookkeeping for the cannabis business and commercial properties. This task required weeks of uninterrupted time. I would normally be helping Brennan at the marijuana farm. I enjoyed the lighter work assignment. I worked in our home office, which had a street view. It was after lunch when something caught my eye. My gaze at the computer transferred to the window. A dark-colored truck was parked on our half-circle drive. Shortly after, a knock on the front door followed.

I came down the front entry stairs, noticing two men. I couldn't quite figure out who they were. My mind raced as I kept my focus on the front door (glass and decorative metal). One of the men was dressed in tactical gear. The other man adjusted his jacket. His jacket had an acronym on it. As I neared the front door, I noticed it said "OSBI" (Oklahoma State Bureau of Investigation). My heart sank, and fear engulfed me as I opened the front door. The man in the jacket began talking, but I was no longer present. I snapped back into the conversation as he repeated, "You may want to leave the house; we are here to secure the house." My husband and his partner Texan had been pulled over. They were in marijuana-related trouble. For some reason, my gaze kept drifting towards the man in tactical gear. I wasn't sure if he thought he would need to use the tactical gear, but it was clear that he was prepared for anything.

All at once, my head filled with questions and thoughts. Then, I reentered the OSBI agents' statement, suggesting I may want to leave. I realized I had nowhere to go and informed the OSBI agent. He agreed I could stay in the house. He said it may be awkward, to which I replied, I do not have a place to go. I went back into the office. I went into a state of numbness and into periods of mental hysteria. The two OSBI agents came inside and settled in the kitchen/living room area.

Within the next hour or two, more local law enforcement arrived. They stayed downstairs in the living room/kitchen area with the OSBI. They would periodically go outside. Upon the arrival of one law enforcement officer, I asked where my husband was. He informed me Brennan and Texan were released from the police. He asked me, "Have you not heard from him?" I said, "No, I have not." He relayed he thought Brennan was going to come home and grab clothes. I did not reply. I wondered why Brennan would grab clothes. I asked myself over and over, *Where is Brennan?*

My state of numbness turned into anger. I knew Brennan was somewhere in the community. Then I thought, *Oh dear, is Brennan on the run?* I went back to the office and sat down. I stared out of the office window. Questions replaying in my mind. Then I saw

Brennan's blue Ford Raptor do a drive-by. He drove by on the intersecting street. Seeing Brennan do a drive-by was like pouring gasoline on a fire. I became furious. At that time, there were two to three law enforcement vehicles in the driveway. The vehicles were not all marked. I thought Brennan must be waiting for the house to clear. I went back into a state of numbness.

As no communication attempts were made, anger grew. Anger surfaced frequently as minutes, then hours passed, and no word from my husband. The daylight was fading into night. More law enforcement officials arrived and departed. I heard the doors open, and men entered and exited. I could not be certain what was going on downstairs. They seemed to be waiting. I felt emptiness and complete abandonment. Brennan had done something illegal and did not have the human decency to check on me. I could not believe Brennan had not called me. I wondered what he was doing. I began to believe he must be on the run under these circumstances. I wondered what kind of husband would ignore his spouse. I contemplated grabbing an overnight bag and leaving him. I ran through scenarios, and I decided to sit and wait.

Around the fifth hour, there were seven to nine members of law enforcement present. Some were in uniform, and others in street clothes. As I came in and out of numbness, I heard them laughing and talking. I remember the normalcy of their conversations. They laughed and talked about everyday conversation topics. I knew my conversations would not be normal going forward. I already felt our lives were forever changed. I wondered when I would laugh and talk again (be normal).

Finally, a man entered the house. The officers were manning the door by that time. I noticed they all stopped what they were doing. It got quiet as they ended their conversations. I heard multiple footsteps on the wood flooring coming in my direction, then up the stairs. Finally, they stopped at the office where I sat. The lead investigator arrived with a search warrant. He provided a copy and explained what was happening. Soon after the explanation, all the officers dispersed within the house. They began the search process of the entire property. They had paper bags and boxes, putting items of interest inside. It was like I was watching a scene from a movie. Now, I was the person in the movie. I was uncertain about moving around in the house or going to the bathroom. I did not want the officers to think I was hiding anything. I felt like I better not make the wrong move, or I would be accused of tampering with evidence.

Shortly after they started searching the house, I received a call. I did not recognize the number but answered the call. A man very hesitantly and quietly said, "Hey Ash, how are you?" At first, I did not know who it was. Then, I realized it was a person from Brennan's circle, the Camel. The name suited him because he was always thirsty. I immediately asked where my husband was, but he did not answer. The Camel asked if I had company. At that moment, I knew he was aware of the situation. He knew what was taking place in the house. The officers were all around me searching. I rudely said, "Yes, there are people here. They are right here!" Camel shut down the call as I demanded he have Brennan call me.

Despair surfaced when one of the officers in the room said, "You haven't heard from your husband?" I sensed the officer realized I was hurt and upset. I was speechless and could only respond to the officer by nodding my head no. Six hours passed, and my husband had not considered my wellbeing. I suspected Brennan was not on the run after the phone call. Brennan was most likely with the Camel or in communication with him.

I was overwhelmed with emotions. I went to the lead investigator and asked if I could leave. I needed fresh air. I saw a movie scene as I walked through the house. It was the drug bust scenes so often noted in movies. I saw officers open drawers and look through cabinets. They placed items in boxes and bags. I felt like I stumbled into the middle of a crime scene as I witnessed search efforts in each room. The lead investigator approved it but explained they had to search my vehicle first. The lead investigator signaled to an officer. The officer followed me to my vehicle. I grabbed my purse, leading him to my garage. It took a few minutes to conduct the search of my vehicle. He finally gave me permission to leave. The search of my vehicle felt degrading. I felt like I was the one caught doing something illegal. As I drove, I went back into numbness and felt unsettled. I decided I would not return home because I felt abandoned. Normally, taking a drive and listening to praise and worship music would create peace in me. That night, I could not be soothed by the drive or music. The thoughts and questions were so loud and chaotic. I knew I was wasting time in the vehicle and drove back home.

Somewhere between 9:00 p.m. and 10:00 p.m., the Camel called back. He wanted to know what was going on. I rudely demanded (I am sure I used profanity) to know where Brennan was. The Camel replied in a quiet voice, "He is right here." Brennan finally got on the phone. Brennan was also quiet and subdued sounding. I started in with questions as soon as I heard his voice. Brennan cut in and wanted to know if the police were in our home. I relayed the police were gone, and he said he'd head home. Within a few minutes, Brennan arrived with the Camel. He informed me he was pulled over by the police. He further explained they confiscated his phone and had no way to call me. Brennan explained what had taken place earlier that day. Brennan and Texan got caught conducting an illegal sale of fifty pounds of marijuana.

Brennan and the Camel began talking about what to do next. They started looking through the house, evaluating what was missing. I discovered while he and the Camel talked, they went to Walmart earlier. In fact, they purchased a temporary phone. I asked why he didn't call me. Brennan said he did not know my phone number. I thought, in the world of social media, he could not find a way to reach out to me. I was extremely disappointed and hurt. I felt he had total disregard for what he had just put me through.

Brennan was visibly shaken, nervous, and in a state of confusion. Brennan apologized, but I could see he was thinking, worried, and in a state of disarray. Brennan only focused on what took place in the house. He voiced aloud when he noticed his cash was seized. He was surprised the marijuana stored in the extra bedroom remained. The marijuana was not supposed to be stored in our home. Brennan and the Camel decided to remove the marijuana product from our home. They loaded it up and delivered it to the marijuana grow.

Upon their return from the grow, Brennan spoke to someone on the phone. Then, he said he needed to leave and meet with them. I was upset and adamant that I would not stay alone in the house. Brennan told me to go to BFF's house with the Camel. It was getting late, and I was already ticked off; now this. I did not know why he had to go immediately and leave me behind.

While Brennan was gone, I visited with BFF and his spouse. They were kind and supportive. We discussed what happened to Brennan and Texan. The Camel began sharing the worst of outcomes in these kinds of situations. Fear, on a level I had not ever experienced before, entered. The fear was ignited and spread like wildfire with each word. I was worked up into a frenzy. I do not know if the Camel was giving me a heads up or using scare tactics. No matter the reason, it made things worse. The Camel said these people (the customers from the bust) will kill you if they think you did them wrong. The Camel added it was odd that Brennan and Texan were released to go home. The Camel relayed it would be quite suspicious to the customers and organization they represent.

I was terrified, and BFF and his wife could see my fear as they expressed empathy. They offered to let me stay with them, and I declined. BFF retrieved a semi-automatic shotgun and loaded it. BFF said I could take it home and keep it as long as I needed.

Brennan finally made it back home, and I drove back to the house. I hysterically began sharing what the Camel told me about the danger we faced. We both were in shock and scared. I voiced that I did not want to stay in our home and discussed going to a hotel. We decided to stay home. We did what we could to get our nerves settled and went to bed. I usually go to sleep within minutes of laying my head on the pillow. I could not go to sleep as questions, events of the day, and Brennan's actions went through my head. I was terrified now and was also upset with Brennan. I didn't know what to do. I decided if he was not remorseful or sorry, I would walk away immediately. After some time, the fear subsided enough, and I finally went to sleep.

The gates of your greatest breakthrough
are formed from your greatest struggles.

Bill Johnson

Chapter 4

———— ∞ ————

Wait, Who Are You?

Train up a child in the way he should go,
And when he is old he will not depart from it.

Proverbs 22:6 (NKJV)

I always read this verse from just the parent's perspective. Now, I see from both the child's and parent's perspectives. This is one of the significant messages from my story. The importance of training your children or loved ones. You will not always be readily available to them. I can't think of a better gift to give. The gift of equipping them with the tools necessary in life. The tools will be engrained deep within them. No one can take them away. Life, for me, might look drastically different if I hadn't been equipped. I had been grounded in a firm foundation. Jesus is the foundation. I faced multiple traumatic events in a short timeframe. I didn't realize the importance of training a child until I was back on solid ground. During the traumatic events, I was operating in what was ingrained in me from childhood. I didn't do it gracefully or immediately. The tools within me had to be remembered, retrieved, and dusted off.

Last summer, I gazed at my first grandchild. He is a beautiful, healthy baby boy. I reflected on our family history leading up to his arrival. I doubt my son or his wife realized what occurred just in my lifetime. There is much to ponder leading up to the arrival of this beautiful gift from God. History always contains pain and suffering. However, if you look closer, it is all wrapped with God's love, grace, and tender mercies. I wondered if my kids would ever think about how they came to be. I hope they see the beauty in how God works all things for good.

> *I will give thanks and praise to You, for I am fearfully and wonderfully made; Wonderful are Your works, And my soul knows it very well. My frame was not hidden from You, When I was being formed in secret, And intricately and skillfully formed [as if embroidered with many colors] in the depths of the earth.*
>
> Psalm 139:14–15 (AMP)

From the moment you are born, your life has many moving parts. You navigate down paths that vary from easy to treacherous. I would say my life was average until I hit my forties—if there is such a thing as an average life. I experienced a decent number of unforeseen circumstances. I've dealt with problems that accompany being human, imperfect, a spouse, a parent, a daughter, an employee, etc.... I have a twin brother, and we were born to a fifteen-year-old mother.

Shortly after we were born, we were placed into the Department of Human Services (DHS) custody. We were placed in multiple foster homes. I hold no ill will, resentment, or unforgiveness in my heart regarding the circumstances we faced as infants. I had a choice to focus on abandonment and rejection or on the greater good. I chose the good! No matter what happened in our infancy, I have always had an overwhelming sense of thankfulness.

I read court documents and DHS records surrounding our circumstances and conditions. One might wonder how I could be thankful. It's easy, and I can sum it up in one word—life! It was our birth mother's decision that ultimately mattered. She chose to give us life. On our original birth certificate, we did not have a father listed. I believe he was not present in our lives, so his support may or may not have existed. I am grateful to anyone who encouraged our birth mother to continue with her pregnancy.

Our birth mother could have chosen the termination route. She faced so much at a young age. I'm not certain, but I can only imagine abortion may have crossed her mind. If not initially, perhaps after she discovered she was having twins. A baby is a huge responsibility at any age and socioeconomic status. Our birth mother would have double crying, feeding, and diaper changes, to name a few. Double everything from birth to adulthood. I am so glad she found it in her heart to continue with her pregnancy.

The State of Oklahoma's records contained various information about my brother and I. Including interesting details along with information about us that was sorrowful. How frustrating the situation seemed. Attempts failed in placing us in a forever home or replacing us with our biological family. Ultimately, each setback was part of God's plan. Our destinies were being orchestrated.

I knew you before I formed you in your mother's womb.
Before you were born I set you apart and appointed
you as my prophet to the nations.

Jeremiah 1:5 (NLT)

My brother and I were children of the state until our second Valentine's Day. We were twenty months old. I was informed by my mom (she's not an adoptive mom; she's my mom) that she received a call at work. The caller had news about a boy and girl, a set of twins. We were available if they wanted us. However, they needed to be in the state capital by 4:30 p.m. I believe she excitedly accepted and hung up. She immediately quit her factory job. My dad carried the mail for the United States Postal Service. This was before cell phones, and they somehow tracked him down. They lived approximately three and a half hours away and had no time to spare. They arrived on time, and we were joined together as a family.

My mom said upon returning home, people from the church and community rallied together. They filled our home with everything a parent would need for a twenty-month-old boy and girl. I get tearful every time I share our story. I visualize God's provision and love being extended through each person. Normally, it takes weeks, if not months, to prepare for additions to the family. Preparation for us took place during their drive time. The church and community gathered everything necessary for the expecting parents.

God's love was manifested through so many people in acts of love, generosity, and support. God's love was demonstrated in acceptance of my brother and me. We were so blessed to remain together. The responsibility of twins (double responsibility) was accepted by strangers. They didn't know us, yet they loved us as their own. The fact that we were loved so much by our new family and complete strangers is enough to melt your heart again and again.

This one movement of God is incredible. God simultaneously made way for helpless infant twins and a couple praying for a family. It's worth ruminating on how helpless we were. We (my brother and I) couldn't pray and lacked awareness of our situation. Yet God took care of us. It is written He dresses the lilies of the field, and He cares for the wildflowers, so He will certainly care for you. It also asks why we have little faith in Matthew 6:28–30.

Interesting side note: My mom and dad had a baby (my sister) the following December. My parents had three children aged two and under in one year. My parents were open and honest with us about being adopted at an early age. I appreciated them for sharing the truth. My parents gave my brother and me different legal names during the adoption process. Our birth certificate reflects those names. We also became known to family and friends as Sissy and Bubba.

And we know that for those who love God all things work together for good, for those who are called according to his purpose.

Romans 8:28 (ESV)

My mom and dad grew up and were both raised around the home we were brought to. My dad served in the United States Navy and worked for the Postal Service. My mom worked in medical settings, and at times, she didn't have to work. My dad supported our family, and my mom's income was supplemental. We were loved and adored by our parents, grandparents, and family members. We grew up on a dirt road called Tanglewood Lane. We were fortunate to have lots of kids, and we always had a ballgame going. There were twelve to fifteen kids on our road, mainly boys. We grew up outdoors and in the country.

My family was a God-fearing family. We were members of a small non-denominational church, Glad Tidings Church. Our parents were not perfect by any means, but they loved Jesus. My parents were strict and didn't waiver when we broke the rules. They taught us to always tell the truth, or the consequences would be worse. That instilled the importance of honesty. I learned even when it's tough, to always tell the truth. I feel that, in being honest, there was always a gentle mercy that accompanied the consequences.

If there was a love that stood out the most in my life, I would say it was my grandmother's love. My grandmother was so loving, understanding, gentle, and peaceful. I don't know if anyone in my life has ever been as proud of me as she was. She continually praised me and would brag about me to everyone we met. I was embarrassed when she did it, but inside, it was building confidence. Something about that made me feel special and loved. I miss having that kind of love and support.

Our family attended church regularly, and they also attended home church (small group settings). I had no idea what was being instilled in me at such a young age. God's word was being planted in my heart; I was being trained up. My parents worked hard to provide for us and taught us to do the same. My mom was especially hard on us girls, telling us to finish school, get careers, and never depend on a man. That was a good lesson. However, it created a super independent attitude in me.

When we were in high school, we moved an hour away. Moving as a junior in high school was rough. I lost friends and my identity. No one knew us. I felt lost initially because I was an outsider. I also knew it was an opportunity to reestablish who I was. I could even be a better version! While I adjusted to the change, softball and work kept me busy. My first job was at a popular fast-food restaurant. That job taught me customer service skills, and the managers modeled amazing work ethics. I adopted the work ethic that was modeled. I met a lot of people working there.

When I was a senior in high school, I faced my first real obstacle in life. I was pregnant and expecting a baby shortly after graduation. Teen pregnancy was a very humbling experience. It brought much shame and embarrassment to me. I worked at the fast-food restaurant until a day or two before delivering my son. I believe being pregnant while working was more embarrassing than going to school. I felt the customers stared in judgment, more so than students at school. I was probably self-conscious. I was thankful for the support from my parents and family members throughout my pregnancy. My family offered their support right away.

I married my first husband (the father of my sons) the day after I graduated high school. We began life together. I was blessed with wonderful in-laws. They were supportive and deeply rooted in God's word. I had a strong desire to beat the odds we faced as a young married couple. We had a new baby, and many said we wouldn't make it very long. I love a challenge, so I wanted to beat the odds placed on our marriage. It wasn't easy or without difficulties. We learned from our mistakes, and after time, we moved along.

My firstborn (KZ) is full of personality. KZ will talk to anyone and light up every room he enters. KZ had loving family members who stepped up when I needed help. I had a hectic college and work schedule. I finished nursing school, and my husband was in law enforcement. Eleven years later, we had our second son, Kale (Road Dog, named by his grandpa). We decided we would have no more children. Kale, my youngest son, is a gentle giant. He's nearing six feet five inches and still in the growing years. Kale was as quiet as a mouse and slow to warm up to people for years. In high school, Kale came out of his shell. I hear he talks too much at school, like his brother. For some strange reason, my boys think they are comedians and have been called class clowns. I think they got that from their uncle Bubba.

Despite the obstacles we faced early on, I was proud of our accomplishments thus far in our lives. My first marriage ended after twenty-two years. At the time of our divorce, KZ had his own home, and we co-parented Kale. My son's dad worked well with me in meeting our youngest son's needs. He and I accommodated one another's needs and adjusted our custody arrangements as needed.

Chapter 5

———∞———

Underneath the Tip of the Iceberg

God can restore most things that were stolen. God will redeem anything that is so broken it cannot be restored. Redemption means recreating as if it were never lost.[2]

I'd seen illustrations of the tip of the iceberg in relation to success. People see a person's success at the tip. Underneath was their blood, sweat, and tears. Our situation would be a good example to use as a reference. The tip of our iceberg was that Brennan did something illegal. That was the visual part, the easy part. Brennan's actions created damage that branched out into our family. The damage affected other families as well. At the time, the damage seemed to affect only Brennan and Texan. However, that was looking at the situation from one perspective. As time passed, I gained an understanding of the extent of the damage. Repairing the damage would be a lengthy

---

2   *Prophesies, Prayers & Declarations Breakthrough*, Shawn Bolz.

process, and repair would be almost impossible. Damage occurred to the business and business relationships. It impacted so many aspects of our life. One could not possibly comprehend unless they took a step in our shoes. Brennan would receive legal consequences. That was a cakewalk compared to what was on the horizon (or underneath the tip of the iceberg).

Brennan and I were numb and in a state of disbelief for the first few days. Brennan had forgotten it was Valentine's Day. He got a Valentine's card for me at the last minute. We were just going through the motions. We were not paying attention to what was going on. Scare tactics began the night Brennan got into trouble. The scare tactics continued through messengers, or as I refer to them, "the shade." We were told we were being watched. We noticed there were strange vehicles parked near the house. I am certain we were told this for one reason. Brennan and Texan went home the day they were busted, and the others went to jail. They were caught selling fifty pounds of marijuana illegally. Going home appeared extremely suspicious. We were told not to talk to anyone and watch our backs. My life had never been threatened. I didn't know what to think. I did not know how to process the threats. Sheer terror struck me deep inside. I felt stomach acid in my stomach as it burned continually. I woke up each morning tasting bile in my mouth. Most likely from the overproduction of acid while I slept.

We had no way of knowing if threats were fear tactics or real. Neither one of us had been in this kind of situation. Indescribable fear gripped me on a level I had never known. The closest experience I can use to explain is a childhood experience. Going into a haunted house was terrorizing. As a child, the terror was real even though it was a staged haunted house. Another example is when you experience a serious near miss, accident, or injury. The fear transmitted shock waves through my entire body. Each time, the fight or flight feeling kicked in. My fight or flight was triggered frequently. I was triggered inside the house and in public. I felt it was only a matter of time before danger appeared. During a fight or flight response, you experience an adrenaline rush. Your survival instincts kick in, preparing for a fight. My body responded to the triggers by dumping adrenaline and cortisol into my system. Soon after, I realized I was safe. Exhaustion soon followed, leaving me with very little to no energy. Brennan, even though he didn't outwardly react, became more vigilant in day-to-day tasks.

We were continually on guard. Frequently looking behind our backs and over our shoulders. The slightest variation from normal was suspicious and triggered fear. Brennan and I devised a plan in case the death threats came to fruition. We stayed in our master bedroom most of the time. The plan was formed from that location. There were two doors in the master bedroom. One door led to the back patio, and the other into the house. My side of the bed was closest to the door leading into our home. I was concerned about being in the line of sight. I considered asking Brennan to switch sides of the bed. I was torn—I also wanted to keep an eye on the hallway.

I remember not being able to watch TV. I could not focus on a movie due to fear. I couldn't quit staring down the hallway. I noticed every light flicker. I turned my attention to every noise inside and outside. Prior to the threats, I never noticed the neighbor's dog bark. Now I heard every bark. Each dog's bark was a trigger for fear. I thought that at any moment, an attacker would appear. I became sensitive to the sound of vehicle exhausts. I heard vehicles on the nearby roads and music playing. I worried about each instance and if someone was sneaking into the house. I felt constant fear in the bedroom because I was the closest to the door. However, I wanted to see what was coming. I wanted the extra seconds to react.

I had a handgun on my nightstand, and Brennan had one on his. We decided once we heard an intruder, I'd grab my handgun and cell phone. I would roll to his side of the bed and then ease onto the floor.

I would kneel next to the mattress and dial 911. Brennan would roll off his side of the bed, grabbing his handgun. He would roll down to the floor and then grab the semi-automatic shotgun stationed underneath the bed. Once we had our positions, we would wait for intruders. We practiced this drill to get positions and timing correct. I feared my hand would be clammy. I recognized a potential problem opening my phone, so I created an easier passcode on my cell phone. Just in case my fingerprint wouldn't work fast enough.

Writing this now, I wonder where my sound mind was. What was I thinking? Why did I stay in that kind of environment? How could I allow this? I was so distraught about the threats of being killed. The terror was almost too much to bear. I can't believe I was planning something so gruesome. I was preparing for a gunfight. The morbid thought of escaping alone crossed my mind. I knew I would run and leave Brennan behind if needed.

Even though we planned and practiced this scenario, I was not comforted. I told Brennan I would call ADT. I requested the removal of the old alarm system because it didn't work. We had a new system installed. The installation of the ADT alarm system may have helped some. It didn't remove most of the worry and fear. Brennan bought door lock reinforcers for every door downstairs. The reinforcers provided additional security. I felt a little more at ease once the reinforcers were installed. The doors were made of solid wood. The reinforcers created more trouble for intruders. It would be a noisy effort, which provided the signal to move! The additional warning time could potentially allow an escape without gunfire. The extra time might allow us to exit through the patio door. I kept an extra pair of shoes beside my bed in case I needed to run.

Due to COVID-19 and distance learning, we had an odd custody arrangement. My son was with his dad at that time. I dreaded the call to my son's dad. I waited a few days before I called him. I didn't know what his reaction would be. I finally called and informed him of what happened. He remained calm for the most part, which is how he normally reacted. He firmly said our son would not be coming back. He said, at least, until he knew things were safe, to which I agreed. He had no idea what kind of safety planning had taken place in our home. He shared a few things. One stood out, and I remember it clearly. It caused me to momentarily reflect upon myself. He respectfully said, "Ashley, I don't care what you do. But that man has put my son's life in danger. I don't want my son there, and quite frankly, I'm surprised you even want to be there!" The call ended, and I went into deep thought. Feeling guilt and shame on top of the numerous other feelings. I was upset, and I figured this would all be behind us in three to four weeks. I was so far off! I think Brennan believed the same thing. He told me to tell the school my son was sick. I ended up telling them the truth, keeping it vague. The school was so accommodating. They allowed my son to participate in distance learning for as long as needed.

WHITE VANS

As minutes, hours, and days passed, warnings from "the shade" and concerned people flooded in. The warnings contained details of the danger we faced. Some had good intentions in their words of warning. However, when they shared horror stories, it was as scary as an actual threat. I believe they wanted me to take proper precautions. Perhaps it was an effort to make me take a step back into reality. I feel they only wanted to shed light on the unsafe situation. I will never forget some of the messages and threats. They were the kind of threats you hear in movies. Some examples were, "Brennan, you messed with the wrong people. These people are bad. You better not run, or they will kill your family. You better bulletproof your vehicle. They have been to your house. They are watching you. They will hang you from trees. They will cut your head off with a butter knife." I realized these may have been made up. Some may have been from a movie or TV show. Again, we had no way of knowing the truth.

One story a person shared wasn't gory but had a lasting impact. It created a fear trigger, activating an immediate fight or flight response. The story was about a well-known drug organization. This drug organization drove white vans. Allegedly, they would kidnap people. The person explained they were never seen or heard from again. In addition to the kidnapping information, they added a true story. They shared a local missing person story. The person got involved with the wrong people. This added more fear and worry.

I don't know how my cardiac and gastrointestinal systems held up. It was hard to get a handle on the symptoms. The terror, anxiety, worry, and confusion were relentless. My heart raced along with palpitation, followed by shortness of breath and then chest discomfort. My stomach suffered the most. It has always been sensitive to stressful stimuli. The scare tactics, threats, and horror stories played over and over. The repeat button had been set in my mind. I became hypervigilant in my normal daily activities. I always looked around for things that didn't seem right. The continual focus on the potential dangers triggered stress. My stomach would feel nervous, then a gnawing sensation. Then, a stomachache caused me to lose my appetite. On the worst days, I thought I was having a heart attack. Nothing relieved that kind of pain. I don't know how I avoided a perforated ulcer.

Now, the site of white vans was a fear trigger. From that day forward, I noticed white vans everywhere. I must have seen thousands of white vans. Each time, I experienced the shock wave of fear. I was on pins and needles each day, especially when Brennan left the house. I went on the lookout like a guard dog. I went from window to window and door to door. Looking for suspicious activity or things out of the normal.

A long time ago, I witnessed a person in a drug-induced paranoia state. I call it "methed-out" state. I had never been around a person in that state. They convinced me someone was outside. Only to find out later that they were on drugs. There was no one outside. Now, I was that person pacing around. I was full of fear. I believed it was only a matter of time before someone appeared. One day, in my paranoia, I saw a white van in the neighborhood. I was about to lose it. I called Brennan right away, telling him what I saw. He agreed to go check it out. Soon after, Brennan returned. I was relieved to hear there was a white van parked down the block. The man appeared to be doing construction at a neighbor's house. Afterward, I was embarrassed. I said to myself, "Get ahold of your mind and quit overreacting." That was easier said than done.

Elijah Prayed, Open His Eyes

One day, I was home alone, pacing around in a paranoid state. I played through scenarios of being ambushed or gunned down. I began to think of the best hiding spots in the house. Even the not-so-obvious hiding spots in closets and under staircases. I explored and discovered multiple attic spaces. I decided to retreat to one of the attic spaces if I had time. I felt it would allow me time to get a call out to 911. I figured it would take an intruder a while to find me. Our home was over 6,000 square feet, with a lot of living space to cover.

In the middle of my strategizing, I was hit with anger. I had the boldness to enter from out of nowhere. I thought, I'm not going to be rushed inside my home and gunned down. I decided to go outside and catch the trespasser. This was the old me, the fighter. I grabbed the semi-automatic shotgun from underneath the bed. I went to my garage and pulled my vehicle out. I positioned my vehicle facing the road traffic. There, I camped out on our half-circle driveway. I watched for the slightest suspicious activity.

I watched the road traffic for a bit. Just as quickly as boldness hit me, so did the fear. I remember talking to God about who this drug organization was. I told God how dangerous they were. I'd surely be outnumbered. I wondered how God was going to protect me. I started to pray, asking for God's protection, and then heard a gentle voice reminding me of the story of Elijah and the servant in 2 Kings 6:16–17 (NIV): "'Do not be afraid,' the prophet answered. 'Those who are with us are more than those who are with them.'... 'Open his eyes, Lord, so that he may see.'" I remembered this story! The servant saw what physically surrounded them with his eyes. But the Lord opened his spiritual eyes. The servant saw an army with chariots of fire on their side! I asked Father to show me too.

In the blink of my eyes, I looked up across the street into a large open field. There was a gigantic angel in a chariot. The angel in the chariot covered the entire open field (half a mile wide and deep). The angel was facing our home. The angel was outlined in bright yellow fire, like the sun. I was awestruck. I'm sure my mouth fell wide open at the majesty of the angel. I heard the Lord say, "You are protected." At that moment, I had a knowing and reassurance. It didn't matter what the enemy looked like. It didn't matter how many they were because I was protected. I instantly felt peace and comfort. I pulled my vehicle into the garage and went back inside. The comfort and peace I received from God's promise carried with me thereafter. I still had scary moments. I recalled this moment after each scare. I found an unexplainable peace each time I focused on God's promise.

POST-IT NOTE

I became very agitated and disappointed with Brennan. He did not do anything about "the shade." They continued coming around, delivering terrifying messages of death and danger. I voiced to Brennan that his lack of action wasn't right. I asked him why he allowed it. His only response was he thought the threats were not real. Real or not, it was upsetting to me. I imagined what my dad would do in the same situation. There would be no tolerance if my mother was being subjected to messages so threatening. I could not and still don't understand why he did nothing.

I eventually took things into my own hands. I decided to stand on God's word. Shamefully, I should have done that initially. I did not want anything entering my house unless it was from God. I wrote down a verse on a Post-it note. I placed it near the primary door we used. The blue-green post-it remains in my possession today at my new location. I simply wrote, "I cover my doorpost with the blood of Jesus." "The shade" came by shortly after placing it near the door. "The shades" message seemed to shift during this visit. I had gotten so tired of the threats. I lashed out and said, "You tell those people to come on, face me like a man." In a different demeanor, "the shade" replied something like, "Oh no, they won't come into your house." I was confused. Previous messages contained no advantage to us. In fact, we were advised to prepare for the worst. "The shade" didn't stay long and left quickly. From that point forward, no one else entered our home with fear tactics or threats. I firmly believe this was because of the power of the blood of the Lamb!

Chapter 6

———∞———

Into the Abyss

Meditate on what God says—our testimonies remind us of what the Lord has done. Every work of what He's done is a prophecy with those with ears to hear... (I heard it in a message.)

Then those whose lives honored God got together and talked it over. God saw what they were doing and listened in. A book was opened in God's presence and minutes were taken of the meeting, with the names of the God-fearers written down, all the names of those who honored God's name.

Malachi 3:16 (MSG)

Burdens began to reveal themselves each day. To name a few, the uncertainty of the future, financial instability, and my son was not with me. Not to mention, the fear of being murdered continually lurked around. I was mentally, emotionally, and physically checked out. The best way I can describe the feeling is the way a movie depicts a person in or near an explosion. A person who has been near an explosion is suddenly jolted and impacted by extreme pressure. An explosion is said to be around 784 miles per hour and can travel up to twelve miles. A person may experience "shell shock" following the blast. I felt like I had been in an explosion, even though I hadn't been. I was alive but in a daze. I could see but was not aware of what I was looking at. I could hear, but the conversations and sounds were muffled. Someone may have been talking to me, but I had no idea what they said. There were multiple occasions I heard my son say, "Good talk." That meant one of two things. He either asked me something, and I didn't respond, or I wasn't engaged in his conversation. I went through the motions during the day but not really paying attention. This went on for months.

We didn't realize it, but our problems were just getting started. Brennan's business partner, BFF, consulted with an attorney immediately after he got busted. We all three rode together to the attorney's office. Brennan signed over managing member duties to BFF. Brennan did not want BFF, Texan, and the Twins to suffer any consequences. Brennan was willing to do whatever was necessary to protect the partners and marijuana businesses. Brennan, at the time, had been receiving a comfortable amount in weekly distributions. The distributions came from their new marijuana drink business. Their new marijuana drink business unexpectedly took off and was doing well. Brennan explained if we continue to receive the weekly distributions, we would be okay, financially speaking. One of his weekly distributions was more than I made in a month as a registered nurse.

A couple of weeks after Brennan's traffic stop, our distributions were cut in half. Then, it ceased two weeks after the cut. BFF stopped distributions and cut off all communications with Brennan. No explanation was provided to us. The business partner(s) locked Brennan out of the marijuana grow property. The sudden distribution withdrawal was unexpected. It created more stress and uncertainty about our financial security. We lost our primary income source. Brennan was sharp when it came to finances and planning. He said we would have to watch how we spent money. He said we would be okay for at least a year. At this time, we still thought the problems would be settled in a few months.

A few weeks after the distributions came to a halt, BFF sent Brennan an ultimatum. BFF suggested Brennan sign over the title to the delivery van. If not, he would no longer take care of the payment and insurance through the company. Brennan did not respond to the ultimatum. As promised, BFF delivered the van to our home. BFF withheld our weekly distributions and added this business debt and responsibility. Brennan was not happy, and I'm sure he was hurt by the actions of BFF. There were two company vans, one in each of their names. We didn't know what was decided, only that we gained a van payment. Brennan understood he would no longer make business decisions. Brennan no longer wished to be a part of the businesses and awaited a settlement proposal.

I ran into BFF twice at his wife's medical clinic. BFF explained he couldn't have contact with Brennan, sending a buyout offer through me. BFF also relayed he had our weekly distributions. He explained he wasn't speaking to Brennan and didn't know how to deliver to us. BFF didn't offer to give me the distributions or set up a time to pick it up. BFF voiced concerns about Brennan's legal matters and how it would affect the partners. I responded that Brennan wanted out, so it should work out for all. I relayed the offer to Brennan, and he scoffed at the low offer.

Brennan sought legal advice approximately two months after the traffic stop. Brennan was excluded from company activities and denied records. He filed a lawsuit for company records in hopes of learning the value of the company. He ultimately sought a fair offer. We learned there was not a fair setup during the injunction lawsuit. There was nothing we could do as far as lost distributions (income).

Brennan's legal counsel advised him to follow the process to prevent damages to his partners. However, there was nothing in place to prevent the damage we faced. We were informed these types of civil cases could take years.

Over the next several months, Brennan voiced to me how much BFF's lifestyle drastically changed. Brennan described BFF's lifestyle prior to the marijuana drink business. Now, he described in detail the difference. If what he shared was accurate, I understood Brennan's anger. It was hurtful to hear and then witness each new purchase or vacation. My eyes watched old things turn new. It stung, knowing we were headed for tough times. I felt, if this was the truth, it was a heinous act on behalf of BFF. He knew marijuana distributions were our primary income source. Brennan continually encouraged me and himself by saying, "The truth will come out." "For there is nothing covered that will not be revealed, nor hidden that will not be known" (Luke 12:2, NKJV).

As we moved forward into spring, we were dealing with the ramifications of the traffic stop in our own ways. The death threats were the most worrisome to me. I was not comfortable with the gun battle planning, installation of the ADT security system, and the door reinforcers. I felt unsafe and unprotected throughout the day, but it was worse at night. I wasn't sleeping well and asked Brennan to reassign one of the marijuana employees. I asked if he would allow one of the workers to watch the house at night. He didn't ever act or even respond to my request. I felt disheartened because he didn't acknowledge my fears.

Everywhere I went, even stepping outside the house, I considered the potential for danger. I scoped out the landscape and exit routes just in case someone was there. I watched my mirrors in the vehicle, constantly aware of the vehicles around me. My husband bought two Tasers and two cans of pepper spray. Brennan and I always carried a handgun wherever we went.

At one point, I remember thinking, *I will not be kidnapped and tortured*. I refused to go out in the ways people described to me. I remember asking someone and researching if I could get a flash grenade. I wanted to purchase one, and I would always keep it near me. I learned that was not an item a person could just buy online. I also thought of ways I could end my life should I be suddenly caught off guard. I pondered what I could do if I was kidnapped. I know the anatomy of human body and the areas vital to protection. I thought of deadly things I could do to someone in the event I faced an attack.

I couldn't believe I was thinking about how to hurt someone or disable them. I realized if it came down to survival, I would survive. I was not tougher than a man. It was of utmost importance to move quickly and strike fast. That would be my only chance of survival. As I typed this, I could only shake my head at myself. I wondered what I would have said or thought about another person if they shared this with me. I told a few people about some of our safety planning, and I'd laugh or make a joke about it. They all replied, "Ashley, that is not funny," in a reprimanding way. It was only then, for a moment, that I would reflect and think, *This isn't right*.

I discovered you never get an "It's all clear" notice if or when the danger is no longer valid. Therefore, the fear of being murdered, attacked, or kidnapped was continual for months, causing me to become unwell. At bedtime, after Brennan went to sleep, I would turn with my back toward him, crying to the point of sobbing. I prayed each time I felt overwhelmed. There were times I had no words and had no idea what to pray. Sometimes, my prayers were one word: "help."

I asked God to help me, and soon after, I felt myself being surrounded by peace and comfort. It was truly unexplainable how peaceful I felt in those moments, and without an ounce of understanding. One night, after praying, I received an image of myself in a violent storm. I saw a glimpse from heaven's viewpoint. I looked straight down from the skies, and there I was in the eye of the storm; I was kneeling with my face towards the ground. I was enclosed in an *impenetrable sphere of peace and protection.* The debris of the situation (enemy weapons and attacks) whirled violently around me. Nothing was able to come near me or harm me in that sphere. I knew God was watching and listening and that He loved me.

> *Do not be anxious about anything, but in every situation, by prayer and petition, with thanksgiving, present your requests to God. And the peace of God, which transcends all understanding, will guard your hearts and your minds in Christ Jesus.*

Philippians 4:6–7 (NIV)

Approximately six to seven weeks after Brennan's traffic stop, he was finally charged with felony drug trafficking. A few weeks after that, Brennan was served in response to a civil lawsuit filed by the District Attorney's office. It was a forfeiture civil suit for the cash and items seized from our home. We were relieved in a way when my husband was charged. Brennan and Texan were not arrested or charged at the traffic stop. "The shade" made us aware of how suspicious that was to a drug organization.

The news of a local, well-known professional man charged with felony drug trafficking spread like wildfire. A concerned citizen alerted the local news station, and it aired immediately. Someone was not pleased with the initial news report. The following evening, another story headlined the news in more detail. The person who reported was an insider. They provided business details to the news station, which was only known by the partners. Many hadn't heard of Brennan's drug traffic stop, as there were no charges until now. The local news filled thousands of homes with the details. The local news also raised awareness on social media. People from all walks of life chimed in with their thoughts and opinions.

A few people reached out to me after seeing the news. Most weren't judgmental and were respectful and supportive. Of course, some reached out and didn't have nice things to say. Some questioned my decision to support my husband. The bravest asked me if I was involved in the drug deal. I answered those who asked, thinking at least they asked and didn't assume.

To fill the day throughout the spring and summer, Brennan and I worked around the house and on his commercial properties. We both worked hard at the grow over the past several months. Now, I felt unproductive as there was no work to do. Most days, I couldn't tell you what I said or did because I was not present. I felt a huge void in my life. We went through the same motions day after day. We slept, worked a little, sat around, and discussed the what-ifs. I know we both had numerous worries, thoughts, stresses, and emotions underneath the surface. We never discussed anything except his business or how badly the partners were treating him.

We began to have disagreements, and patience with one another decreased. Brennan scolded me one week for visiting my son for three days instead of two. I was completely at a loss for words. He was upset because I was wasting money. He said I was putting too many miles on my car for making three trips. I was juggling my son's physical therapy, allergy shots, and regular visitation during these unforeseen circumstances. I couldn't believe Brennan became so upset. In my opinion, he created this problem. I saw the yellow school bus every day when it passed our home. Each school bus sighting was a sobering reminder I didn't have my son. Each time, the guilt, shame, sadness, and feeling of loss hit me. I couldn't believe Brennan had no compassion. Not an ounce of understanding in the way I felt about not having my son.

In the late summer, Brennan began to voice we would be better off if he were dead. He told me if he had an accident in his vehicle and died, it would not be an accident. I felt he insinuated vehicular suicide. I rebuked him and explained suicide would put all his burdens on me and his family members. He began to leave the house for hours at a time and wouldn't tell me where he was going. He would not answer phone calls or texts. He left his phone behind on a few occasions. I was a basket case worried about him. I didn't know if he was coming home or committing suicide.

Not long after that, we were walking one evening. Brennan told me he understood homicide-suicide cases. I was speechless as my mind raced. I wondered who the homicide victim was. I firmly explained to Brennan that if he made any more comments about suicide, homicide, or accidents, I would call a mental health facility. I would have him admitted, and I would also call his parents. All my worries and concerns seemed to go to the back burner with his disturbing comments. I wondered if he realized this was an additional fear added to my plate. I had more than plenty to deal with currently. Now, I was worried about his safety and for mine. I knew I needed to watch him more closely. I ordered two GPS tracking devices with magnetic cases and always kept one on his truck.

Summer break was coming to an end. I had been without my son for approximately six months. The first week of August, my son's dad and I discussed the status of Brennan's criminal issues. The criminal case and other civil cases were not near closure. He felt it would be best if our son stayed with him and started school where he was now. He voiced that difficulties may arise as the cases come to closure, and danger may still be an issue. Deep inside, I agreed even though I did not voice it. I agreed because Brennan and I were still on the lookout. Every time we went outside, we had a gun, taser, or pepper spray. Even though I agreed, it was like a punch in my gut. I cried out loud after I hung up the phone. I cried as I tried to explain to

Brennan what was decided. I could tell Brennan knew I was deeply hurt as his facial expression turned to concern. Brennan instructed me to do something about it if I did not like what was happening. I was completely lost and overwhelmed as I tried to figure out what my options were being unemployed. Brennan suggested I get a job and get a second household, adding he couldn't support two households.

After I pulled myself together, I knew I would have to get a job and a secondary home. I recalled a discussion I had in the vehicle with Brennan and BFF the day we went to the attorney's office in February. I sensed a looming dilemma between my role as wife and mom. While we were at the attorney's office, I asked the attorney what a custody battle would look like if Dad didn't want our son back in our house. The attorney nodded his head, gesturing it wouldn't be favorable. I was presented with a decision that no one should have to encounter. But here I stood with the burden of choice between son and husband, and it glared me in the face. I heard no other options or ideas from my husband. He only made it known he couldn't afford two households. He never acknowledged my idea of him finding a place to stay or secondary locations. I chose my son, and I felt overwhelmed. I knew a lot of work had to be done to secure a second home.

One of the toughest lessons a Christian can learn is how to trust and praise God in the uncertain times. When we are in between the promises and its fulfillment. It's a powerful act of spiritual warfare to stand in the middle of conflict that's unresolved and cause your spirit to rise and give thanks to God.

Bill Johnson

Sermon "The War in Your Head"

Chapter 7

———————∾——————

The Downward Spiral

The passing of time was strange. Some days, time moved at a snail's pace, and other days, it rushed. It had been six months since the drug bust, and the school year was quickly approaching. My son was not returning home. I frantically started planning how to secure custody and provide a home. I was concerned about being hirable. I wasn't sure how Brennan's criminal charges reflected upon me. I worried how a second location would work with my spouse (who carried an element of danger).

I don't believe my husband contemplated how his reckless act affected others. He became easily offended when people voiced their perspective of his crime. My husband would not extend forgiveness or mercy but expected it immediately. He made me feel horrible for the idea of a second location. He made me feel I was asking him to do the unthinkable by living in another location. I explained couples live long-distance all the time and make it work. He would not hear of the possibility of living in two locations. He accused my son's father of controlling his life. My husband only viewed things from his perspective.

After a short while, my husband excused his criminal behavior. He said people need to get over it because he would receive punishment.

Brennan began to minimize the act of trafficking fifty pounds of marijuana. He stated, "I just sold a bag of herbs. It was just a bag of oregano." I knew how he would have reacted if his son's stepdad had done this. I could imagine the outrage he would have demonstrated. I wondered how Brennan would've handled the same situation if it was reversed. Would there be hesitation if I created a wedge between him and his son? Would Brennan stay with me? What if I was the one who did this? What if I was the one who distorted our life so drastically that it became unrecognizable?

A drastic turn of events initiated a meeting with the Choctaw Nation Family Services Department. The turn began after I was offered a job and began looking for housing options. This caused no small stir with Brennan, and we began to argue more often. My husband's fuse was extremely short. He'd burst out in anger with the slightest disagreement.

One evening, after a walk, we sat outside in the pool house. Our conversation transitioned into arguing. In anger, he grabbed a plastic water bottle, wadding it into a tight ball. Brennan wound up and threw it as hard as he could towards me. The bottle hit my left forearm before flying into the flower bed. After he hit me with the bottle, he went back into the house as I remained seated. I began thinking about what took place. My feelings were hurt, and then I became alarmed. My husband physically meant to harm me. I called my brother, Bubba, and told him what happened. Bubba informed me that the action was considered an act of domestic violence. I didn't want to call the police for something so minor. He suggested I start recording Brennan when he gets angry. He warned me to be careful around him, explaining it could get worse.

My husband came back outside approximately thirty minutes later, saying I was a baby. He implied it didn't hurt, then denied throwing the bottle at me. When I discovered Brennan's lack of remorse, I relayed the information I had learned moments before. I told him I could call the police, and he may go to jail. He was barefoot, and I told him to go put on his jailhouse shoes. Brennan went inside and didn't come back out. I sat outside for a while in deep thought.

Two days later, we spiraled out of control. That day will always stick out from my timeline. I reached a boiling point I had never experienced. It was an early evening, and I was watching TV in our bedroom. My husband approached me in an agitated manner, demanding my vehicle key, but I refused. I knew he was fuming because he was red-faced. He immediately left the bedroom, and then I heard him go outside. I went to the laundry room to get a peek. I wanted to see what he was scheming. I saw the delivery van parked in front of my garage, barricading my vehicle. Brennan entered his garage, and I went outside to address him. I asked Brennan to move the van or give me the keys, but he refused. I ran inside to see if the extra keys were in the drawer, and they were gone. I ran back outside, and it appeared Brennan had thrown keys into the yard. He entered his truck and started the ignition. I hurried to the back of his truck and stood. I began yelling, "Stop!" refusing to give up my ground.

I felt this situation drifting out of control; as I yelled, the truck sensor sounded, and there was no compromise on-site. I remembered I had my phone and flipped the video on to record. As I yelled stop, my husband continued to ease back in reverse. I lost my footing due to the weight of the truck being forced onto me. I fell, and Brennan stopped the truck, putting it in park. I got up and walked to his side of the truck. I told him to move the van or I would call a wrecker. When he realized I was out of the way, he backed out and fled the scene.

I watched his blue Raptor race out of the driveway and fled west. The same direction he did the drive-by the day the police secured the home. It was a deeply disappointing feeling, and then anger overshadowed all feelings. I realized if danger arrived, my husband had left me with no transportation. I looked at the van and looked around for keys, hoping for a solution. I couldn't figure out a way to move the van and called a wrecker service. They stated they would come out if needed but were busy. I relayed to them I would think about it and call back if I still needed them.

I paced around in anger and went back to my garage. I assessed a gap I could potentially squeeze through. I believed the gap was large enough to get my vehicle through. I was so mad and decided I would have rammed through the gap. I didn't care if it damaged my car, garage, and van. I made it through the gap without a scratch. I went inside to grab my handbag only to realize my handbag was missing. Brennan stole my handbag and had hidden it. The handbag had my wallet, money, identification, and things for work. I needed it. Brennan had taken my handbag before and hid it for days. I hoped that wouldn't be the case this time. I grabbed two handguns I believed were equal in price. I would use them as leverage if needed.

I called a lady I used to work with, and she met me in town. I also called Bubba and relayed to him what happened. Both Bubba and the lady said I needed to leave. They felt my husband was dangerous. Bubba advised me to call the police and file a report and a restraining order. Bubba said I did not have to pursue charges, but it needed to be on record. I called the police and told the officer what happened, sharing videos and photos of my injuries.

I finally cooled down enough and went back home. I figured we would sleep it off and talk about it later. Upon arrival, I discovered I was locked out of our home. All doors were locked, and I presumed he engaged the reinforcers from inside. The front door didn't have a reinforcer, so I rushed around to get a look at the door. My hope quickly disappeared as I noticed a metal cable wrapped around the door handles secured with a padlock. I lost my mind at that moment, taking a quantum jump into a rage. The lady was still with me during the discovery. She tried reasoning with me, asking me to walk away. I ignored her and went to the backyard into the pool house.

I stared at potential tool options, noticing the bolt cutters were missing. The only tool I thought would be useful was the sledgehammer. I decided to carry out an extremely destructive act. I would destroy the beautiful, expensive, oversized glass windows running along the back of the house. The glass ran the distance of the living room, dining room, and hallway. A little sanity must have remained because I came up with a less destructive option. Plan B was devised for the front of the house instead of the back of the house. I was positioned and ready to carry out plan B. Then, I heard the voice of the Lord speak through the lady. In a calm but urgent and loving tone, she said, "Ashley, this is not you. Don't do this." The lady's voice was like my grandmother's tone, which had a loving rebuke. I had only heard the loving rebuke tone a few times while she was alive; it contained power. I was instantly gripped with conviction during the rage. Somehow, it was enough to cause me to rethink and stop the retaliatory behavior.

My husband refused to work with me or let me inside. Finally, he agreed to allow the lady to come inside. He said she could grab some clothes and items for me. Brennan also made a deal: he'd give my handbag back in return for the guns. The lady entered the house; they had no idea what to grab. They went back and forth between my closet and me as I stood outside watching. It was nearing 11:00 p.m. I needed everything to get ready for work the next day. I remember looking in and seeing how pleasant and calm Brennan presented. I also remember the look on the lady's face—it was so empathetic. I felt so bad that I brought her into the middle of our issue. When Brennan made me stand outside, it made me feel like I was an intruder, a criminal, and a stranger. I felt powerless as I stood there in disbelief.

Then I remembered my car had a panic button! I pressed the panic button so the neighbors would notice. It was not long before

Brennan pleaded with me to turn it off. I told Brennan I would disable the alarm if he let me in the house. I desperately wanted to grab my own things. He agreed and let me in the house. I disabled the panic alarm as promised. I tearfully gathered clothing, shoes, makeup, and a few toiletries. Deep despair hit me as I was almost finished collecting my things. I realized when I exited my home that I was officially homeless. My husband made it clear he wanted me out and offered no other options. The despair intensified as I loaded my belongings into my car. I hoped my husband would stop this or ask me to come back inside.

After I loaded my things, Brennan had to retrieve my handbag in town (undisclosed location). He told the lady he would meet her in five or ten minutes. I was instructed to wait for my belongings at her house. As soon as Brennan took off, I acted like I drove off too. I did a U-turn going back into the house. I retrieved the vehicle title and a few more of my items. I went upstairs and unhooked the wiring to the Wi-Fi. I grabbed a bottle of water and took a drink as I entered our bedroom. I became maddened knowing my husband would return to our comfortable bed and I had nowhere to go. I poured the remaining water onto the bed. The lady offered to let me stay with her, but I had burdened her enough and declined. I stayed at a local hotel. I was devastated and confused at how we came to this point. My mind raced a million miles, and I finally went to sleep.

WHEN THE DUST SETTLES

The next morning, I woke up in a strange room, immediately remembering where I was. I realized the downward spiral was real. As I got ready for work, I understood this was an urgent matter that added to my sea of problems. I could not afford to stay in a hotel. I went to work heartbroken, with swollen eyes, and homeless. I was technically on the streets with only a handful of personal items from my home. Somehow, I found reasons to be thankful that morning. I had a bed, matching work clothes, the right makeup to be presentable at work, and coffee.

During my first break, I went to family services at Choctaw Nation. I was fortunate to find out that Choctaw Nation Family Services would help with a hotel during this unimaginable circumstance. They reserved the hotel for a week, and I diligently began seeking housing options. Their domestic violence department made me aware I was eligible for free counseling, rental assistance, utility deposit assistance, a family advocate, and an attorney if divorce is needed. I only heard housing and utility assistance because I was primarily concerned with housing.

I stayed in the hotel the entire week, never hearing from my husband until Saturday night. He called, saying he was checking on me, wanting to know where I had been. He spoke at great length about the problems and my actions. As he questioned me and my behavior, I tried to comprehend the purpose of his phone call. I asked myself how he could overlook his behavior, having no regard for my safety and well-being. I didn't engage or question him. I knew I would be moving to a second location. I needed to move out in peace and have access to my things in our home. I had to keep my composure and bite my tongue for the sake of peace. The next day, Brennan said I could come home, and I returned. I never received an explanation or apology. My husband vowed to love and protect me, yet this series of events was far from that. So much of my trust in him was lost after that incident.

The following week, I consulted with Legal Shield about the dos and don'ts of moving to a second location. I wanted legal advice on needing things versus taking things to a secondary location. I wanted to conduct myself fair and under the law. The attorney asked me if there was anyone who could lure Brennan out of the house. The attorney said that would be the best time to move, given the recent events.

I found and secured a home this week. Shortly after, Brennan and I were walking one evening. He notified me he was leaving at four the next morning. He was going to Tampa Bay to watch the Dallas Cowboys. Then, to Naples, Florida, for the remainder of the weekend. I was in shock because he was leaving in less than twelve hours. I was also puzzled and hurt because he voiced we were supposed to be watching how we spent money. Ultimately, I knew this was a blessing in disguise. The landlords had reached out that week, letting me know I could start moving things in. Brennan was aware I could start moving and explained that's why he made vacation plans. He didn't want to be around when I moved.

I asked Brennan for the password to the security cameras and Wi-Fi that night. He didn't provide and left the next morning at 4:00 a.m., no goodbye. I had no access to Wi-Fi or the security system. Without Wi-Fi, I had no ability to call or text in the house. I was already scared due to the dangerous situations (threats). If danger appeared, I wouldn't be able to see security cameras or get a phone call out. This sounds horrible, but at the time, I wondered if Brennan was trying to have me killed. I told a few people what was going on, and they insinuated the idea. Each relayed how convenient an alibi would be if something happened to me. Given the circumstances, the idea was not that far-fetched. Fearing the worst, I reserved a hotel room while he was out of town.

I began moving things into the rental, working on it through the weekend until late at night. Brennan told me when I moved to take everything with me. I did my best to get my things out of the house. On that Sunday evening, I had moved most of my things. I did not have any furniture except an end table and my son's bedroom furniture. The rental was empty, with scattered trash bags and totes containing my belongings. I didn't want to take furniture until we discussed it together. Brennan returned from his vacation late that night. He started calling and texting at 11:30 p.m. and continued until

6:00 a.m. the next morning. My husband threatened divorce and to call the police. He threatened to cause me to lose custody of my son. Brennan was upset, and I was confused because he knew I was moving.

The following week, we discussed the circumstances at my new location. I believed we would figure out how to make a secondary location work. I informed my husband I was sitting, eating, and sleeping on the floor. He offered the small kitchen table and chairs, living room furniture, and a bed. Brennan explained he needed to clear the house out because he planned on putting it on the market. The following day, my husband changed his mind. He promised those items to his daughter, who had a fully furnished apartment. I was appalled and deeply hurt because he knew my situation and hers. He made an intentional choice to leave my son and me on the floor to sit, eat, and sleep.

From this point forward, a vicious cycle entered our lives. It was a continual cycle of being loving and then hateful. Some weeks, we agreed to work things out, then always back to divorcing. Brennan refused to support my preference to have my son in the secondary location. The support meant being tied to the area for my son's entire high school years. I knew it wasn't an ideal situation, and my husband desired to move away. I felt our marriage slipping away. We still faced all the other problems. I do not believe my next discovery was accidental. Light was shed onto and exposed my husband's betrayal. I was completely devastated.

Each night after work, I helped my husband with tax preparation. While searching for tax forms from the previous year, I made a grave discovery. I saw my husband's search activity, and it was crushing. I saw specificity in what my husband was currently seeking. I saw immoral relationship sites I didn't know existed. I saw pornography sites, which hurt, but knowing the type of female he desired cut deep. There were searches for age-specific women in precise demographic areas. I sacrificed so much for this man, standing by him and supporting him for months. All the while, he sought ungodly relationships with women. I was heartbroken and felt my heart shatter into hundreds of pieces. I called Choctaw Nation the next day and asked to speak to the attorney because I wanted a divorce.

I'd never considered what a pit was until I was afflicted with illness (described in the first chapter). That illness was the most challenging experience I'd ever dealt with. I hated being in that place, "the pit." Now, I was back in the pit. This pit was deeper and darker than I had previously experienced. I tried to articulate how awful my pit was, and there were no words, so I found a few descriptions online.

It is a place of destruction (Isaiah 38:17), a dark and deep place where the dead are without strength, forsaken by the living, and forgotten by God (Psalm 88:3–6). There is no thanksgiving, praise, or hope there (Psalm 38:1–8).

A pit was made and then covered lightly over, served as a trap by which animals or men might be ensnared (Psalm 35:7). It thus became a type of sorrow and confusion from which a man could not extricate himself of the great doom which comes to all men, of the dreariness of death (Job 33:18, 24; Job 28:28). To "go down to the pit" is to die without hope.[3]

Imagine falling into a pit and tirelessly screaming for help. Every time you believe you have figured a way out, you fail. The exhaustion (physically and mentally) eventually shuts you down. Leaving you with a sense of being defeated, stranded, hopeless, and grief-stricken as the idea of escaping the pit ceases. I was in this state and was desperate to escape.

One of the contributing factors to my delay in escaping the pit was my lack of proper coping skills. The lack finally caught up with me. I was trained early in life not to cry and tough it out when I was

---

3   *Pit—Bible meaning & definition—Baker's dictionary* (no date) *Bible Study Tools.* Available at: https://www.biblestudytools.com/dictionaries/bakers-evangelical-dictionary/pit.html.

hurt. An example would be when I played softball and got hit by a ball. I was taught to tough it out or walk it off. Growing up, if we cried about an injury, there had to be an injury severe enough to back it up. Otherwise, we were made to feel weak and lacked toughness.

This was a good lesson to toughen us up and not to cry wolf. Unfortunately, it would have a detrimental effect on me years down the road. I not only fielded physical pain but also fielded emotional and mental pain and injuries. By "fielded," I mean I would catch or pick up the pain and quickly release it, never addressing it. I would not admit it hurts because I felt this would reveal a weakness in me. I don't remember crying in my twenties and well into my thirties because of the guard I built around me.

My problems were insurmountable, each changing form as they snowballed. They snowballed because I never addressed them. Just when I thought my life was challenging and difficult enough, things began to deteriorate. The weight of fear, guilt, shame, embarrassment, loss, and confusion were heavily bearing down on me. I never imagined it would be possible to experience more turmoil, pain, confusion, and suffering, yet here it was.

As I found myself back within another filthy pit, I still had hope. God delivered me from an illness pit, and I knew He was faithful. This pit was deeper and darker; escaping wouldn't be the same and seemed impossible. However, His promises are for every situation. The following paragraph couldn't be more truthful: being saved from the pit was an amazing demonstration of God's love.

The pit or dungeon was a commonplace of punishment in the East, and very dreadful it was, as the case of Jeremiah illustrates (Jeremiah 38:4, 9). To be doomed to the pit was often to be left to a slow death by starvation; *to be saved from such a doom was regarded as the greatest of all deliverances*. Hence, it was used.[4]

4   Pit—Bible meaning & definition—Baker's dictionary (no date) Bible Study Tools. Available at: https://www.biblestudytools.com/dictionaries/bak-ers-evangelical-dictionary/pit.html.

I held onto God's promises in the pit. I had hope and confidence it would come to pass without understanding.

Not a word failed of any good thing which the Lord had spoken to the house of Israel. All came to pass (Joshua 21:45).

The Fisherman

Previously, we learned the beautiful relaxing fishing day had taken a turn. Now, a battle was at hand, figuratively and literally. Subsequently, the fisherman would be faced with decisions that would impact his future. The fisherman had toxic snake venom pumping throughout his circulatory system. Interesting facts, "A blood cell in the average person travels through the entire body in about one minute. This incredible velocity moves 83 gallons of blood an hour.[5] Panic would certainly cause the heart to beat faster and the venom to be pumped through his system at a higher rate. The fisherman needed a team of medical professionals to limit the devastating effects.

We are the sum total of our decisions: we are free to choose, but we are not free not to choose, nor are we free to choose the consequences of our choices. Adrian Rogers says, "First you make your choice, and then your choice chooses you" (from the message *It Is Decision That Determines Destiny*).

The fisherman could remain on the ground and wonder how, what, and why this happened. He could project blame and focus on all the contributing factors leading to the injury. Things he could focus on are his poor shoe choice or lack of coordination, causing the fall. The slow driver who created the perfect time to encounter the snake. He could sit and stare at his injury, observing the wound change rapidly. Totally oblivious to his body's reaction to the snake venom. He may allow the agony and pain he is experiencing to consume him. The fisherman must be aware he needs help; inaction will create more complications. Diverting his focus on the would've, could've, or should've(s) most certainly would delay his medical attention and care. The fisherman acted promptly, made the wise choice to seek medical attention.

---

5   Institute, June, 15, 2018.

Chapter 8

———— ∞ ————

Ashley, You're in Denial

THE THREE WISE MEN

*He lifted me out of the slimy pit, out of the mud and mire; he
set my feet on a rock and gave me a firm place to stand.*

Psalm 40:2 (NIV)

I prayed this verse during my health crisis and now in this current
mess. I didn't form any ideas of how God would provide a firm place
to stand. I only trusted, then entered The Three Wise Men.

The Three Wise Men I refer to are my attorney (legal),
counselor/advocate (professional), and godly counselor (God's
truth bearer) from my church. The expertise of each one was a
powerful medicine. The medicine they poured into me was vital to

my well-being. Through a family services program, I was provided an attorney, a licensed professional counselor, and an advocate. I made an appointment with my godly counselor, Pastor Terry Brown. The Three Wise Men and my efforts to diligently seek God's word redirected my course. It initiated the scale removal from my eyes. The team's counsel, guidance, and God's word activated the ascension to higher ground. I began to receive awareness of my situation.

And immediately there fell from his eyes as it had been scales: and he received sight forthwith, and arose, and was baptized.

Acts 9:18 (KJV)

I reached out to The Three Wisemen after a couple of incidents. Both incidents occurred earlier in the year (a few months after Brennan's traffic stop). My husband did two things within a few days of one another. I was hesitant about reaching out but was concerned. I battled the idea of being viewed as weak but decided to reach out. The first incident was in our bedroom; we were arguing. Brennan escalated more quickly than normal. I saw him pacing as he turned red in the face. He scanned the area around him, and I knew a tantrum or physical act of violence was coming. He focused his eyes on a TV remote. Suddenly, he picked up the remote. He threw it as hard as he could in my direction, shattering when it hit the wall. He immediately said, "You're not saying anything now." I didn't say anything because I was in shock. I worried how I would have reacted if he had hit me.

The second incident occurred in the kitchen. Brennan was standing at the island chopping celery for our tuna, and I was sitting at the bar. Brennan asked me if I had called the exterminator. I replied, "No, not yet." Brennan went on a rant, and I said something sarcastically. I told him he sits around the house all day, just like I do. I said he could call too. My response elicited a volcanic reaction. Brennan started screaming and cursing me. He escalated quicker than usual on this day. All of a sudden, he elevated himself on his tiptoes. He reared back as far as his arm allowed with the knife in hand. Then, he stabbed the granite countertop as hard as he could. The knife shattered, and pieces went flying. I didn't want him to think his actions influenced me, and I just stared at him. Shortly after, he acted like it was no big deal and calmly walked away. I got up immediately after he left the kitchen. I was curious, wanting to know what the knife looked like. I wondered where the pieces landed. I only found one piece ten to fifteen feet away. It was weeks later before I found other pieces. The stab was so forceful pieces were found on the staircase. I am not exact, but it was close to first-floor ceiling level and twenty to twenty-five feet away.

Brennan's eruption into violence was so explosive. I wondered what he would have done if I had been near him. I witnessed how strong and sudden his act was. It was the first time I worried that he would hurt me. I knew I wouldn't respond fast enough to deflect the act should he lash out at me. Brennan and I had engaged in physical altercations earlier in our marriage. These two volatile acts, coupled with death threats, led me to believe I might qualify for family services assistance. I wanted to know, just in case things got worse. The acts also alarmed me enough to seek godly counsel for wisdom and to have someone stand with me in prayer.

Pastor Terry, one of the Wise Men, was familiar with us from marriage counseling. Approximately two months after Brennan got busted, I asked about going back to counseling. My husband declined, which was a hard pill to swallow. I knew I needed godly counsel and encouragement. We isolated ourselves and had very little contact with anyone. We hadn't attended church regularly due to the COVID-19 shutdown. I seriously doubted we would attend church anytime soon since Brennan was charged with felony drug trafficking.

I was desperate for encouragement, wisdom, truth, and guidance. I ended up lying to my husband so I could attend a counseling session with Pastor Terry. I felt awful for lying to my husband. I gave Pastor Terry a summary of what happened, and I don't remember what he said to me. The one thing that I still hear as clear as a bell is when he said, "Ashley, quit talking about Brennan!" I stopped not realizing what I was even talking about or that I was focused on Brennan. Pastor Terry changed the direction of the session. At the end of the session, I felt so much better.

By the third month, post-relocation, I had met with my attorney, advocate, and licensed professional counselor. The counselor, one of the Wise Men, repeated something I heard from Pastor Terry. She stopped me and said, "Ashley, stop talking about Brennan!" When I heard this for the second time, I was in a state of shock, but it caused me to take a step toward awareness. I didn't realize what I was saying and had been talking about Brennan again.

The next reality slap was when my counselor, attorney, and advocate told me I was in denial. They advised me I was in denial about the danger I was in and the relational situation with Brennan. I was informed I was in a domestic violence situation. I didn't agree, which is denial, because I was "tough." There was another reason I didn't admit to my problems. It was due to a statement I made in the past. I bragged about having a gift of discernment. To accept what they advised would be an epic discernment failure on my end. The hardest part was when they discussed domestic violence, and I had no idea what it entailed. I didn't know domestic violence wasn't only physical abuse but financial, emotional, sexual, and mental. I had shame in admitting this because I'm supposed to be smart. To be unaware of this in my life would discredit my intelligence.

I didn't want to believe I was in a domestic violence situation. I would go back to the justification that I wasn't punched, slapped, bruised, or have black eyes. I didn't think I looked like the image of the battered wife that's usually portrayed. My attorney strongly encouraged me to file a protective order with the divorce. She believed I was in danger. I was further surprised when she referred to my husband as a perpetrator—the title seemed so serious. My attorney said the incident when Brennan backed over me was worrisome. I explained to the attorney he didn't slam on the gas and plow over me. She said it didn't matter; he didn't stop the vehicle. I told the attorney I would think about it and get back to her before we filed the divorce. I started thinking about our marriage and what may have occurred pertaining to domestic violence.

During the scale removal from my eyes, a Wise Man asked me if Brennan ever put his hands on me. I recalled a few times but didn't think it met the criteria for domestic—physical—violence. The first incident occurred during the first month or two of our marriage. It took place in my closet when Brennan became upset and was yelling at me. I continued to take care of my business in the closet, and he started escalating. The next thing I knew, Brennan charged towards me, forcefully grabbed my left arm, and jolted me. It was like a parent who grabs a disobedient child's arm. The parents hastily try to get their attention, letting them know they are in charge. I had a wooden hanger in my hand, and I reacted by yanking my arm from his grasp. I squared up towards him with a fist in one hand. The wooden hanger was raised high in a defensive position, ready to use. Brennan instantly stopped and walked away. He didn't say or do anything else.

Some days later, we laughed about it. Brennan told me I had a look in my eyes that cautioned him. I told Brennan I was ready to fight him. I knew he was stronger and tougher than me, but I would still fight him. My parents taught us to stand up for ourselves. We were taught to never back down from a bully. I was prepared to fight back even if the outcome wasn't favorable. I realized now I dismissed this incident so easily, without a second thought. Brennan didn't explain his actions; therefore, no apology was received. I felt the issue was settled because he walked away and understood I would engage if needed. I also felt a sense of victory because he walked away and was cautioned by my look.

I continued to scan our history for potential signs of domestic violence. I noticed a pattern in our arguments (verbal, mental, and emotional). Our arguments went on for two, three, and four hours at a time, ending late at night and never resolved. At the conclusion, he would not sleep in our bedroom and slept upstairs for days. The arguments ended with him telling me to get out of his house and later demanding my wedding ring. He threatened to move my things out the next day while I worked if I didn't comply. The next day at work, I was a basket case, wondering if my son and I were homeless.

I recalled an incident occurring earlier in our marriage (physical, emotional, mental, verbal). We argued for hours, and I refused to give my wedding ring back. My husband went upstairs, and I stayed in our master bedroom for the night. I was sound asleep, suddenly awoken by the bedroom light being flipped on. Then startled by the loud screaming and cursing. I opened my eyes and gathered my thoughts. I realized Brennan was in a rage and was holding a wet wash rag. He came straight towards me as I lay in the bed. He began scrubbing my face with the wet wash rag. I was mortified and in a state of confusion for a split second. He shouted, "You are an ugly Indian girl. You covet makeup; you better wash your face, or you will get zits."

The shock of the situation was only for a moment. I immediately transitioned into fight mode. I reacted swiftly by throwing my legs up around Brennan's neck, securing a firm leg lock (between my thighs). I used my body weight to pull him down from standing to lying down on the mattress. I wasn't sure what he was capable of at this moment. Out of pure survival mode, I told God, "I am not letting go of Brennan until he passes out." I had Brennan's neck squeezed tightly with my thighs.

His face color began to change shades, from anger red to blood constriction red. Oxygen deprivation manifested as hints of blue appeared on his face within seconds. I felt myself gaining higher ground in this attack. Then, I felt Brennan tap out (the universal sign to quit) on my leg. I loosened my grip and released Brennan. He got off the mattress and then quietly scurried away into the darkness of the hallway.

I lay there in disbelief. I took a few deep breaths, calming myself. I tried to process the incident; however, it was imponderable. Suddenly, I thought, *What if he comes back?* I started planning my next moves in case he came back to retaliate. I decided I was going toe to toe with him if he returned. There would be no mercy. I was hyped up, doing Rocky fighting prep moves (in my mind). I was as mad as the old saying, "An old wet hen."

My husband didn't come back, and I eventually went to the bathroom and turned off the lights. I was ignored after that fight for days. Eventually, we got back in good humor, then laughed about it. Brennan revealed to me he tapped out because I hurt him. He explained when I threw my legs up, I kneed him in the temple area, causing immediate discomfort and a knot. Brennan pointed to the area on his left temple, revealing the knot. After recalling this event, I went on without an apology. Yet, he wanted me to know I hurt him. Everything about this incident and my lack of addressing his behavior baffles me.

Another incident came to mind. The behaviors, to me, were jaw-dropping (physical, verbal, emotional, mental). It occurred earlier in the marriage as well. We had argued, and I was being antagonistic and didn't give my wedding ring back. That night, my refusal to comply sent Brennan into a tangent. He threw my clothes out of my closet onto the bedroom floor and into the hallway. When I didn't engage, he escalated to higher levels. He began taking all my makeup and hair-styling items from the bathroom. He carried some out of the bedroom and hid. He threw some of the items onto the floor. He noticed I wasn't disturbed by his behavior, and he disappeared for a moment.

Brennan reappeared with my expensive Christian Louboutin handbag. He held it up with one hand and had a black permanent Sharpie in the other hand. Brennan held the handbag up like it was a hostage. He threatened to write on my handbag if I didn't give my wedding ring back. I could only see a scene from the movie Con Air. The scene when Cyrus the Virus (John Malkovich) held a gun to the head of a stuffed pink bunny. Cyrus the Virus told Cameron Poe, "Make a move, and the bunny gets it." I told Brennan I didn't care what he did to the handbag. I didn't buy it, and I didn't need it. He disappeared with the handbag, and I discovered later that he had hidden it.

Holding my handbag hostage was strange. The next event was even stranger. It occurred shortly after the handbag hostage attempt failed. I continued to lay on the bed, watching him. He began to mock me by acting like he was walking in high heels. He pretended he was drinking coffee, calling me a hillbilly. Brennan said all I did at work was drink coffee and walk around in high heels. Brennan had thrown my makeup basket onto the bedroom floor. He leaned over the basket and grabbed one of the lipsticks. Brennan unscrewed the lid and said, "Look at me, I'm Ashley; I covet makeup." He pulled the lipstick applicator out and smeared it onto the bottom portion of his face. I was rolling with laughter on the inside. He had no idea what he had just put on his face. He smeared my MAC matte long-wear lipstick "Topped with Brandy" on his face. It takes an act of Congress to wash it off.

I was entertained by his behavior, watching in awe. This reminded me of the mother in the movie *Mommy Dearest*. I had never seen anything like it in real life. I never responded, and he finally retreated to the upstairs bedroom for the night.

The next morning, I noticed most of my makeup and hair-styling items were missing. He didn't know I had makeup stashed everywhere. I had everything I needed for my daily makeup routine. I informed Brennan I would not pick up one piece of clothing thrown out of my closet. After multiple days, he picked up my clothes and placed them neatly in my closet. After days of silence, I eventually got makeup and hair products back. Some of my makeup was trashed and never recovered. The handbag was returned without a mark on it. I discovered one of my wedding photos (metal art) was destroyed. He had written "Crazy B—" on it with a permanent marker. Sometime later, the writing on the photo was removed. We never spoke of this incident. He never apologized or admitted wrongdoing. I never questioned his destructive behavior. Feeling like I "won" was probably the reason I said nothing. I thought I won because I didn't give the ring back, and he picked up the mess.

I had never thought about financial abuse or what it looked like. I discovered I experienced this type of abuse in our marriage. During a visit with one of the Wise Men, we reviewed a safety plan. She said something that raised my eyebrows. The Wise Man went through a safety checklist. I noted I had already put most of the recommendations in place. The recommendation that raised my eyebrows was to hide a set of car keys. At that moment, something triggered a thought within me. I remember thinking, it's not normal to hide a set of car keys. Yet, I had already hidden the extra set. I quickly justified the action as being normal. Reminding myself why I hid the extra car key.

The week I resigned from my position, almost a year after we married, Brennan bought me a brand-new BMW X4M Competition. It was right off the showroom floor. A few weeks after the vehicle purchase, we had an argument. Brennan was very angry at me for something I mentioned to my son's allergist. It pertained to the wife of BFF and her medical clinic. It was regarding allergy shots and a simple step in the shot process being skipped. Brennan harshly reprimanded me. He said it could cause problems to his friendship with BFF. Brennan became so angry he threw our new pool furniture into the swimming pool. I was surprised he threw it in the pool because it looked like a stagnant pond. He also said something that was so ugly about me. I chuckled when he said it because I had never heard it. Brennan yelled, "Go crawl back into the hole you crawled out of!" I was used to the name-calling. I thought, *Well, that's different*, and smiled.

Shortly after the argument, I realized my new car keys were missing. Brennan hid the car keys as punishment for my honesty with the allergist. I was working with Brennan at the grow at this time. He didn't speak to me and left me behind for a week as further punishment. My previous BMW was approximately three to four miles away. It was sitting on his commercial property with a for sale sign on it. I waited about a week; Brennan hadn't given the keys back. It was a scorching hot day in July, and I took off walking to my vehicle. Brennan was headed home and approached me on the roadside. He offered to take me to my car, but I refused. My feelings were hurt. I couldn't believe he was keeping the keys after he discovered where I was going.

I had trouble understanding my husband's actions. I couldn't think of a reason to withhold the keys for so long. I lost a level of trust in my husband in this situation. I was honest with Brennan and meant no harm to anyone. Yet, he took a harsh stance against me. I called BFF and his wife after Brennan's explosion. I explained what I mentioned to the allergist, and neither was bothered. I relayed their response to Brennan. I was astounded when he didn't change his position. I was thankful I still had my previous vehicle. I began to worry about what was going to happen when I sold this vehicle. I won't have a backup. Brennan kept the keys hidden for approximately a month. After this incident, I kept the extra set of keys in a hiding spot. I never received an apology or acknowledgment that he'd done anything wrong.

The Wise Men took time to explain domestic violence at length. As I shared incidents, they helped me identify the type of domestic violence it met. I forced myself down memory lane, recalling events during our marriage. I knew my husband, and I had a rough start in our marriage. I felt our marriage got better once we started working together at the grow. I explained to the Wise Men some of the incidents I shared were from the beginning of our marriage. They shed light on the current incidents and how it was still a pattern of domestic violence. I eventually began to identify how behaviors met the criteria of domestic violence and a toxic relationship.

I told one of the Wise Men I was accused of playing victim. I worried about receiving that label. The Wise Man looked at me and said, "Ashley, you were a victim. Now, you are a survivor!" I felt encouraged to hear that. I gained knowledge and guidance each visit. I had never thought of domestic violence being anything except a physical beating. I was simply not thinking at all. I decided, after recalling my history, that I would move forward with the protective order. My attorney said she would file it with the divorce.

The Three Wise Men were pivotal in my story. They each provided their respective wisdom, knowledge, and experience (legal, professional, and God's truth). I was completely inept in making decisions or seeing the bigger picture. I had to acknowledge I needed help, and it was imperative I didn't lean on my own understanding. I mentioned it at the beginning of this chapter, and I will repeat it now. I didn't form any ideas of how I'd be rescued from the pit; I only trusted God and then entered The Three Wise Men.

My people are destroyed for lack of knowledge.

Hosea 4:6 (KJV)

Trust in the LORD with all thine heart; and lean not unto thine own understanding. In all thy ways acknowledge him, and he shall direct thy paths.

Proverbs 3:5–6 (KJV)

Chapter 9

———— ∽◇∽ ————

Alone and the Silence

The Lord himself goes before you and will be with you;
he will never leave you nor forsake you. Do not be afraid;
Do not be discouraged.

Deuteronomy 31:8 (NIV)

Once the petitions for protective order and divorce were filed,
life became silent. I soon understood I was completely alone. Before,
even though we fought, I still had someone in my life. Now, he no
longer reached out because of the protective order. The notifications
on my cellphone ceased. No one called or texted me regularly. In my
opinion, being alone and in a foreign place (physically and mentally)
felt like I was a prisoner. I was consumed with hopelessness and deep
despair. Being alone was the darkest and most desolate state I had
ever experienced. I felt miserable and that I no longer mattered or
had meaning in life. People, including myself, used the terms lonely

and alone interchangeably in discussions. I used to think feeling lonely and being alone were the same, but they were different. Being alone is described as a state of being, while loneliness is a feeling.

I went through my life asking how I got to this point. I have no family or friends. Looking back, I noted multiple separations from family and/or friends. There was a lack of maintaining those relationships. I was given up as an infant with no biological family relation. I moved away from my hometown when I was sixteen years old. I got married the day after graduation. I focused all my attention on a new marriage, a new baby, and completing college. I divorced twice, and each divorce resulted in relocation. With each move, I lost my worldly identity and sense of belonging.

I could only blame myself for not having friends. I did not actively pursue new friends. I knew I could ask KZ to be more present; however, that would be selfish. I didn't want to guilt my oldest son into filling the void. I felt his extra time should be spent with his family and friends. Realizing now he may need friends one day. I won't always be around or available to him. A lady spoke at our women's ministry recently regarding our children. She shared on our role to equip them with God's truth and importance of community. She reiterated what I felt in my heart about my children's community. We won't always be there for our kids; their community could play an important role in their future.

During this state, I recalled animals in the wild. Specifically, when a member of the pack strays. The stray member becomes an easy target for the predator. I was the stray member. I was vulnerable and in unknown territory. I frequently lay prostrate on the floor and sobbed. The sobbing spells hit all hours of the day and night. Occurring at work and home with very little warning. I had some control at work, only leaking a few tears. However, in the car or at home, the episodes were ugly crying breakdowns. I dreaded leaving work daily because the rented house was not my home. The unknown environment intensified the foreign feeling. I remember being sick in the past. The anticipation of being home and getting into my own bed was so comforting. I no longer had a place where I felt comfortable or at home. I had no one to talk to, complain to, or cry to. I longed to be comforted and held. The feeling of being home became distant and unfamiliar. For the first time in my life, I felt like I didn't belong anywhere on this earth.

Monachopsis:

The persistent feeling of being out of place and not fitting in. It's the inability to adapt to your surroundings and feeling like you don't belong.

I remember hearing people complain about the chaos of holidays. I thought, *They don't have a clue.* I wanted to scold everyone complaining about having too many places to go on the holidays. They had no idea how blessed they were to have someone. As major holidays came and went, there were no calls asking if I was coming. No one called to ask what I was cooking or what I would bring. It was an empty feeling. I dreaded the question, "How was your holiday?" It served as a reminder of having no one, and I felt ashamed about being alone. I feared the follow-up questions that may accompany me if I told the truth. I decided to respond with, "It was good."

When I wasn't crying, my mind was on one of the hundreds of problems I faced. One of the Wise Men asked me how often I thought about Brennan and his problems. I realized I thought about him or our problems every fifteen to twenty minutes. I thought about it more often initially. After answering the question, I realized I had a serious problem. I couldn't help it and didn't know how to escape.

During one of the safety planning sessions, I realized how alone I was. It was pitiful and depressing. The Wise Man and I reviewed a safety plan checklist. The Wise Man said, "You do have someone checking in on you daily, right?" I had a completely hollow feeling. I held back tears as I nodded my head yes. I knew there was no one. If something happened to me, there would be a delay in discovery. Only being discovered if I didn't show up for work or didn't pick up my son. I kept the Life360 app (GPS tracking app) on. My brother suggested it shortly after Brennan's traffic stop. I knew they could see where I was in the event I went missing. Well, they could see my phone's location.

I was driving one day when I heard an audio message that caught my ear. It hit home and was amidst my challenges and darkness. The preacher discussed the difficulties surrounding suffering. I heard the congregation's amens and uh-hums as they agreed with the preacher. If you think about it, we can all relate to some degree of suffering. Then, he made a comment silencing the crowd. The preacher said, "There is one thing worse than suffering. It is suffering alone!" As the crowd suddenly quieted, I immediately came alive! I said, "Wow, you are so right!" The agony of suffering alone felt worse than physical discomfort. I had family members who were alive and nearby. Unfortunately, they were not involved in my life for different reasons. A few checked in initially, shortly after, disappearing into their own life. I understood that all too well.

I learned that even if someone has a family, they may be suffering alone. I will never assume someone has support when they have living family members. I will remember the significance of daily encounters with people. We have no idea the burdens people carry—they are unseen. People could be in deep, dark pits while they perform their daily functions.

During the lowest of lows, an encounter with a stranger changed my outlook. It took place in the parking lot at work. I was leaving for lunch, and I met a vehicle. As I neared the vehicle, I saw the driver was a lady with salt and pepper-colored hair. We passed one another, and

I noticed she waved at me. I did a half-wave, trying to figure out who she was and why she waved. What stood out about this interaction was her smile. I saw joy in her face as she waved and smiled at me. I thought I must know this woman, but I couldn't place her. Perhaps the woman may have mistaken me for someone else.

Some days later, I saw her in the building, identifying her by the beautiful smile. That day, I returned the smile. Her warm smile had an impression on me. I think about her smile often and how it changed my day in the parking lot. I received a word from the Holy Spirit about her smile. The revelation was about Sarah Abraham's wife. I always wondered what Sarah's beauty looked like because, in Sarah's later years, she was beautiful. The lady's smile was perhaps a glimpse of one of the characteristics of Sarah's beauty.

It was several weeks later, but I shared this insight with the lady from the parking lot. I spoke with her in my office and learned her name was Lisa Harper. I wanted her to know she changed my day and how I'd relate to others going forward. I shared with her about the day she waved and smiled, explaining I was having a horrible day. She had no idea how low my life was. I relayed that her smile gave me hope. I experienced hope through a simple smile, and I thanked her. The smile was a random act of kindness. I recall the impact of her smile to this day.

Adrian Rogers said, "In times of grief and sadness, acts of kindness speak louder than the right words ever could."

The protective order hearing was approaching, and I discussed the process with my attorney. She explained what to expect and what a judge may want to know. She mentioned the term "imminent danger." After the call, I began to ponder that term. I felt like my husband's conduct was egregious and meant to harm me. I'm not sure if I was battling the image of lacking toughness or felt a soft spot for my husband. I was torn about going through with the protective order. Brennan's behavior scared me, but I didn't know if I felt like

I was in imminent danger. Maybe I'm foolish, but to me, imminent danger was someone putting a gun to your head. Perhaps suffering alone was too much to bear, and dropping the order would open the door for communication. I asked the attorney to drop the protective order.

I went by Brennan's a few days later, and he was reluctant to talk to me for obvious reasons. He finally came outside, and I explained I decided to drop the protective order. We discussed only one event on the protective order: the vehicle incident. He claimed it was staged, and he did nothing wrong. I asked him to see it from my perspective, but he stood his ground. My husband never asked me if I was okay after I was knocked down. Brennan explained that day and many times afterward how hurtful that was. I believe the protective order created a barrier between us, and I doubt he ever forgave me for it. Brennan never acknowledged the other incidents written on the court document and never apologized for the behavior.

Multiple times since filing for divorce, my husband explained how we needed one another. He said we needed to work together and get through all the issues. We loved one another and wanted to be together but couldn't get on the same page. I would usually agree to do whatever he suggested. We would get along for a few days or weeks, then return to arguing and isolation. Life would be so good in those few days or weeks. The other days were painful, and we would be in that phase most often.

During the chaos and confusion, I would usually cry until there were no more tears. Lastly (shamefully), I would talk to God. I never asked God why this was happening to me. I never asked God where He was. I never blamed Him. Even though I didn't initiate the chaos, I knew I was responsible. My poor actions and choices, or lack thereof, potentiated the issues.

Adrian Rogers shared there are two kinds of storms we experience in life. A perfecting storm or correcting storm. My storm was a correcting storm, no doubt. I was not in the will of God, and I knew it was course correction. When you are in the will of God and face a storm, it's a perfecting storm. No matter which storm, God is in it with you. God is overall; nothing takes Him by surprise.

Instead of blame, I wanted explanations. I wanted the situation dissected and revealed. I appreciate and desire explanations in all settings. I generally ask lots of questions in life because I want to understand. Whether I agree or not, I move on easily. I received no insight during my suffering whatsoever, and it gnawed at me.

Some months later, I discovered the reason I wasn't getting explanations. The following verse came from a message by Pastor Duane Sheriff. I heard it during his series Immaturity—A Trojan Horse. Pastor Duane mentioned, "A lack of discernment has knocked you down." He referenced this scripture. "There is much more we would like to say about this, but it is difficult to explain, especially since you are spiritually dull and don't seem to listen" (Hebrews 5:11, NLT). Pastor Duane shared we must have an ear to hear to receive understanding. He went on to say that when understanding occurs, change happens. Even if the Lord provided explanations, in that season, I wasn't listening. I was dull of hearing.

I also received more insight after listening to Steven Furtick's message, "Power of a Better Question." Pastor Steven referenced Numbers chapter 13, when Moses sent twelve leaders to explore Canaan. Steven Furtick summarized the message. He said you get dead-end answers to the desert questions (who, what, when, and why). Steven Furtick said desert questions are limiting questions and enemy questions. Pastor Steven went on to say we are to have the faith of Caleb. We are to look at challenges through a positive lens. In doing so, what we see as impossibilities turns into opportunities.

At some point, when there were no explanations or answers, something happened to my way of thinking. I began to think from another perspective. I started asking a different question, "God, what is the lesson I need to learn?" I can't prove this, but it seemed like I heard an answer when I changed to this question. I noticed I would hear something shortly after. It would be something I heard with my heart. Explanations or answers were delivered through audio messages, songs, a person, a book, a church, or a co-worker. Even to the current day, answers to my question, "What is the lesson I need to learn?" still arrive. I love this question now because I realize no matter what life throws at me, it's always applicable to ask, "What is the lesson in this?"

The lesson I learned about being alone was received from a convicting question from the Holy Spirit. I heard it in my sarcastic voice. One day, I was holding a pity party. I cried about how horrible being alone was. All of a sudden, I heard in my sarcastic voice, "Oh, you're alone, *hm*?" I knew exactly what that meant, and I felt instant shame.

When I heard that question, I realized I had never been alone. I knew the Lord had been with me the whole time. Right before my eyes, like a recap of a TV series, I had a flashback in my memories. I saw numerous instances of Him with me. I saw His peace and comfort surround me in the chaos. I remembered the security I sensed in the darkness and unknown. I saw many times how He acted on my behalf. I saw all the people he sent me. I saw on the lowest days when I felt the alone state intensifying, friends, coworkers, and church family would unexpectedly reach out.

From that day going forward, I developed a different response when feeling alone surfaced. Each time I drifted toward complaining about being alone, I reminded myself of two things: the promise in Deuteronomy 31:8 and the sarcastic question, "Oh, you're alone, *hm*?" And I knew I was not alone!

The Lord himself goes before you and will be with you; he will never leave you nor forsake you. Do not be afraid; do not be discouraged.

Deuteronomy 31:8 (NIV)

Which may go out before them, and which may go in before them, and which may lead them out, and which may bring them in; that the congregation of the LORD be not as sheep which have no shepherd.

Numbers 27:17 (KJV)

Chapter 10

———— ⌾ ————

Staring Crow

You might be thinking, *Staring Crow*. Perhaps wondering if it's a story, game, landmark, or none of the above. Creepy or scary is my first thought. From the moment I heard it to now, it means something much different.

I diligently read articles seeking answers on what was wrong with me and how to get well. I carried the burden of our lurking marital failure. I lugged a heavy blanket of guilt around after my husband accused me of abandoning him. My husband frequently voiced he felt like a hostage and people were controlling his life. I knew he battled things I didn't know about. I was consumed with so many emotions stemming from the drug bust, relocation, divorce, new job, betrayal, and being alone.

I was desperate for relief and wanted to address my problems. Unfortunately, I could not pinpoint what to focus on. I didn't like feeling lost, and it was miserable. I knew how to pray and stand for physical healing, but now I asked, "What am I standing for or against?" I was in such a state of confusion, with no idea what I needed to be delivered from. I knew if I could grasp the name of the root problem, I could pray with specificity. However, I only knew the emotions.

One day, I was talking to someone who lost a loved one. They described how they felt after the loss. I didn't say anything, but I wanted to say that's how I feel. I feared I would offend them because I hadn't lost a loved one. I didn't want them to think I was comparing my pain to theirs. At my next visit, I told the Wise Man I believed I was experiencing grief, even though I hadn't lost anyone to death. The Wise Man said, "Yes, you most likely are." The Wise Man explained I had experienced great loss. I felt hopeful after hearing that. Now, I had a name (problem) to focus on. I could tackle recovering from grief and loss. I only caught a glimpse of grief and loss, but I agree with Barry Bennett, professor at Charis Bible College. In a healing class, Mr. Bennett said grief can kill you if you don't move to mourning.

"Have mercy upon me, O Lord, for I am in trouble: mine eye is consumed with grief, yea, my soul and my belly. For my life is spent with grief, and my years with sighing: my strength faileth because of mine iniquity, and my bones are consumed" (Psalm 31:9–10, KJV).

One of the Wise Men asked me a series of questions. I was caught off guard when the results revealed I had PTSD (post-traumatic stress disorder). That diagnosis sounded so severe. I felt like my circumstances were less traumatic than those I knew who had dealt with it. Later that evening, I looked deeper into PTSD. I started with a simple question. What is trauma? Trauma is defined as a deeply distressing or disturbing experience. Now, a follow-up question: What is PTSD? PTSD is when thoughts and memories of traumatic events don't go away or get worse. This can seriously disrupt a person's ability to regulate their emotions.[6] Again, I was hopeful in receiving the information. I knew this was another name (problem) to add to my focus and recovery.

6   *Trauma* (no date) *CAMH*. Available at: https://www.camh.ca/en/health-info/mental-illness-and-addiction-index/trauma.

As knowledge and understanding were deposited, decisions to accept or deny were presented. With acceptance, shame accompanied, but healing was on the horizon. Unbeknownst to me, denials prolonged my healing and victory. The next deposit of information was unanticipated and harder to accept. This deposit caused me to grudgingly look deeper into our marriage and self-reflect.

One of the Wise Men handed me a piece of paper. The paper had an illustration of a cycle, and I noticed it was a continuous cycle. I looked at it closely and saw a cycle of emotional abuse. I gasped as I read it. I saw the events of our life together being placed into each phase of the emotional abuse cycle. (The stages were tension building, incident, reconciliation, and calm.)

I wondered if this type of behavior occurred in my previous marriage. I wondered if I was the problem. I scanned through over twenty years of my first marriage. Nothing came to mind that would fit in this cycle. This caused me to think about things Brennan mentioned about his first marriage. I tried to remember if he'd mentioned anything significant. I couldn't remember anything; only our issues were magnified.

No matter what occurred during either of our first marriages, we were our own worst enemies. Our chemistry seemed to be extreme on both ends. Our love was incredible when we were not fighting. However, when we disagreed, it was a major catastrophe. Once we engaged in a dispute, I stood my ground and defended my stance. My husband would do the same. I don't know if Brennan had ever been challenged to this degree. I like a healthy debate, and sadly, these were the opposite. I thought he might have been at his wit's end in dealing with me.

Ultimately, we had not conquered the ability to compromise during conflict. The oddest thing ever was that we agreed on almost everything. We were agreeable 99 percent of the time in our marriage. The conflict generally arose when I shared my feelings. Once I shared a feeling, an argument ensued, and then chaos followed. Our behavior was perfectly reflected in the emotional abuse cycle.

I was appalled at how my stance in conflict transitioned over time. It went from remaining quiet in an argument to immediately coming out with guns blazing. As intelligent as we were alone, much less combined, you'd think we could have found common ground. This scripture couldn't fit in a better situation than this.

"Pride leads to destruction, and arrogance to downfall".

(Proverbs 16:18, GNT)

My husband shared something strange when we were dating. Brennan told me he went into his ex-wife's house looking for items of sentimental value. He ran across his ex-wife's hate journal, explaining it was a book she wrote mean things into. I asked what she wrote, and he said it was mean stuff and never elaborated.

A few months into our marriage, I started writing down events. More specifically, the wrongs. I believe this was what my husband meant when he said "hate journal." I started writing the events down because I noticed Brennan kept a record of wrongs in his memory. He would recite these during each argument. My husband never put the wrongs completely away. He always pulled them from his memory when there was conflict. The craftsmanship in keeping my wrongs concealed was quite methodical. I never suspected they would revisit me.

In the heat of the moment, I felt defeated when I never had an insult to bring up. Winning the argument became my focus. We both have a fierce competitive nature that rivals one another. I normally have a forgive-and-forget mentality. I believe that is a strength, but in our situation, I felt it was a weakness. I was tired of being landblasted with artillery from our history. Soon after, I had my own arsenal of wrongs to call upon.

I'm certain this was my first detour off the right path. I was reluctant to keep a record of the wrongs. I knew it was written in the Bible that love does not keep a record of wrongs. At the time, if anyone asked me if I loved Brennan, I would have, without hesitation, said yes, of course. However, once I started writing down each insult, it was the opposite of love. Also, keeping a record led to unforgiveness, which opened the door to destruction. Therefore, it was true to say I hated Brennan, and he hated me. Only now, with understanding, I see we operated with hate and pride during the conflict.

The injuries from the insults I inflicted upon Brennan created a reaction I detested. Brennan would ignore me for days and weeks. I'd never been treated like that by my first husband. It was an extremely distressing experience. We would have no contact or communication even while we were in the house. Brennan would not answer telephone calls or texts. The isolation and being ignored were far more painful than the shouting, name-calling, or physical altercations. I tried to explain to Brennan how sickening this made me feel, but he never changed. I knew it wasn't right to go to bed with anger in my heart because it is written, "Don't let the sun go down while you are still angry" (Ephesians 4:26, NLT).

I reflected on my first marriage, realizing isolation and ignoring me were foreign behaviors. I was not accustomed to that kind of conduct and didn't know how to deal with it. I recalled a dispute with my first husband and how he responded. We had a disagreement, and I was upset. I decided to watch TV and sleep on the couch for the night. It was bedtime, and he was in our bedroom, and I was in the living room. I was lying there in the darkness, getting heavy-eyed. All of a sudden, I heard clanging and banging on the front porch. I shot up off the couch and ran into the bedroom. I got under the covers and clung to my husband. I told him what I had heard. Later (not sure if it was that night or the next day), he told me what it was. He admitted he opened our bedroom window, leaned out, and threw a boot onto the front porch. That was the noise I heard. We were over our disagreement the moment I jumped into the bed and clung to him. We didn't stay mad at one another. He never ignored my texts, calls, or me while in the home.

A Wise Man suggested rejection, and I dismissed it as soon as it was voiced. I didn't feel I had been rejected. At that time, I didn't know all the ways rejection could be demonstrated. I only thought of someone asking another out on a date, and the person responded with a rejection. I lacked the knowledge to identify rejection in this setting. Rejection occurred every time my husband gave me the silent treatment. Rejection presented each time he didn't answer a phone call or text message. Rejection occurred when he went to work without me. We did everything together, and each time he left, I was rejected.

I was unaware continual rejection was significantly impacting me. Emotions one experiences when rejected include hurt feelings, loneliness, jealousy, guilt, shame, embarrassment, sadness, and anger. I discovered the stages of rejection were like grief and loss. The stages are shock, denial, anger, depression, and acceptance. This was a constant cycle I had been dealing with, and I had no idea about it. During the silence, rejection was painful and tormenting. The most hurtful part was the person I loved dearly was the one inflicting the pain with intentionality.

Much later, the topic of rejection surfaced, and the idea I may be dealing with it. I stumbled upon Pastor Robert Madu while listening to Steven Furtick's weekly podcast. I was excited to find out Robert Madu was stationed in the Dallas area. I just so happened to be in the Dallas area one Sunday. I eagerly wanted to attend his church, Social Dallas. During my first visit, Pastor Robert Madu spoke on praise and rejection. I recognized the past behaviors and acknowledged it was rejection. I was delivered from rejection. Thank You, Jesus, for deliverance. This message is on YouTube and titled "PR Problems."

It is well worth the time if you think you might be suffering from rejection. One of the main takeaways was rejection is redirection!

As time and distance increased from our separation, my eyesight became sharper. My husband and I were not a loving married couple. I knew the popular love verse in the Bible, yet I operated on my own terms. I sink low even today when I think about it. I knew we weren't obedient to God's word. I felt further conviction because of what I told my husband in my marriage vows. I said I wanted to show Brennan God's kind of love. I felt God must be disappointed in me because I didn't extend His love. I showed Brennan love that even the lost person can extend. Not one descriptive word of love in this passage was present during our conflict.

"Love is patient, love is kind. It does not envy, it does not boast, it is not proud. It is not rude, it is not self-seeking, it is not easily angered, it keeps no account of wrongs".

(1 Corinthians 13:4–5, NIV)

I recognized another detour from the right path. Name-calling, mocking, and belittling me had minimal effect. I had total disregard for those types of insults. My dad had a saying when someone bothered us. He told us to let it (insult) roll off us, like the water rolls off a duck's back. I was trained to do that, and it was helpful advice in life. I was also taught the truth of who I belonged to and who I was in the Lord. The truth kept me grounded when the insults came. I could have been called a table, book, frog, dog, or any curse word. All the words had the same effect on me: none.

My lack of response to the name-calling created more agitation. One day, my husband shouted at me, "Are you just going to sit there and say nothing?" And I did. My husband gave me a nickname "Staring Crow" because I didn't engage. My husband informed me

I was abnormal. He described me as stoic because of the flat affect I returned to his jabs. I quietly accepted it as a compliment.

The enemy recognized the ineffectiveness of name-calling and belittling. He became crafty and shifted the target of the attacks. It wasn't long until a little crack in my armor appeared; the enemy found a way in. Brennan stopped insulting me during arguments. He started to harshly criticize my kids and family. I couldn't overlook the comments about my family and kids. The "Staring Crow" flew the coop and left the region. I instantly went into battle mode when Brennan jabbed at my kids and family. I became ferocious, like a grizzly bear with cubs. Once provoked, I became aggressive, behaving like a wild animal. Being protective and fierce as a grizzly bear isn't the issue unless you are being deceived. I was fighting the decoy the enemy set in front of me.

I experienced a different kind of hurt each time I heard his crude comments. I didn't understand why someone who loved me could take jabs at my family. My family was an extension of me. I never resorted to name-calling towards Brennan or the members of his family. I knew that once it was spoken, you couldn't unhear it. I felt it was a high level of disrespect. I loved and cared for Brennan's family. I feel I brought dishonor to my family due to my lack of action to the hateful words.

I felt like I was taking the higher road when I didn't engage in the arguments. The Staring Crow remained quiet, keeping composure. However, it seemed to open doors to worse behaviors. My husband would escalate verbally and then reach a boiling point. That is when he acted out physically in a rage. I could always tell when he was going to act out physically. He would pace around in a frantic manner. Like the Tasmanian devil in the Looney Tunes cartoon or a dog urgently searching for a place to relieve itself. The quick-pacing movements always preceded the physical outburst. The physical outbursts involved picking up an item, winding up, rearing up onto his tiptoes, and throwing or breaking items. Items he threw or broke were whatever was within arm's length.

On two occasions, he snapped his golf clubs in half, over his knee, at the golf course. I was taken aback, to say the least. The destruction of property is incomprehensible to me. I didn't know what to think about it. I felt like the young lady in the movie Bridesmaids, watching the maid of honor terrorize the bridal shower. The young lady was open-mouthed and oddly entertained, much like I was, to Brennan's outbursts.

I was stunned by the intensity of his physical outbursts. The best way to describe it is a comparison to a character in a movie. The intensity of Brennan's volatile physical outbursts reminded me of a scene in the 2004 movie Collateral. The scene with Tom Cruise and Jamie Fox. The intensity Tom Cruise (Vincent, the contract killer) had in the club scene was exactly what I saw in Brennan's outbursts.

Another bothersome behavior was comparable to a scene from Brothers. Tobey McGuire was in a rage with a female who appeared to be his wife. Tobey's behavior was identical to Brennan's in one of his frenzies. The screaming and destruction of property is not what jumped out and caught my attention. It was when Tobey slapped himself in the face in the middle of the rage. In one of Brennan's outbursts, he was so enraged he slapped himself in the face. I was worried when he did it. I positioned myself in a defensive stance after taking a few steps back. I was uncertain what his course of action would be. I was especially uncertain since he resorted to hitting himself in the face. He did not touch me and kept his destruction on physical items within reach.

I feel the intensity would have bothered most people or created intimidation. At the time, I would have said I wasn't scared. I also know I was in denial. I kept a distance during the outbursts, and I wouldn't have done that if I felt safe. I was apprehensive and should have been alerted. This could have turned into something worse. I couldn't believe how drastically his behavior could change. He quickly transitioned from a bubbly, fun guy to out-of-control rage. He could also go from rage to a completely gentle, calm man in a matter of seconds.

I visited with a counselor briefly after we were married. I felt like I was standing in quicksand when we had an argument. I say quicksand because the concern moved nowhere. I sank deeper into the quicksand as I was berated for past events, not even a current issue. One simple dispute turned into hours of arguing, then ended with isolation or volatile outbursts. I received advice on presenting my concerns to Brennan. The approach, no matter how gentle, would start a three-to-four-hour tirade. I learned I'd rather bury the hurt feelings than listen to a rant. The rants caused mental and physical exhaustion with no resolve. This was not the right way; it didn't bury the feelings. They were being pushed into hiding spots, and at some point, the hiding spots got scarce.

One of the Wise Men asked me a question that ripped the veil of denial off. I was asked what advice I would give another person who shared the same circumstances. The question was staggering because I knew what I would tell another person. I wasn't doing what I would advise another person to do in my situation.

The Staring Crow was my first thought after the removal of the denial veil. I knew what the Staring Crow symbolized from my husband's perspective. It was used to characterize my blank stare and unmoved during the commotion.

To me, the Staring Crow was a fruit of the Spirit. When a Christian is in a close relationship with Jesus, they exude goodness. They live a life with good morals, evidenced by the good fruit. I am not portraying myself as perfect. I walked in the fruit of the Spirit early in our marriage. The Staring Crow used to describe me was self-control and longsuffering. Long-suffering is described this way.

Someone who's long-suffering puts up stoically with discomfort, trouble, or other people's bad behavior.[7]

My director, Aleisha Williams, is a godly woman who shares God's truth in love. Sometimes, the truth was convicting, and other times comforting. Her advice was always consistent with the Word. One of the questions she asked me was what the fruit was in a situation or decision. I began to measure choices and situations by the fruit of the spirit. I wished I had received this tidbit much earlier; perhaps the Staring Crow would have stuck around.

Now, I use the verse below as a tool. The tool helps me determine when I am headed in the wrong direction. I can continually be aware of my attitudes and behaviors. I know if I am not the Staring Crow, I am probably out of line. If I am not operating in the fruit of the spirit listed below, it's time to redirect my path.

> *"But the fruit of the Spirit is love, joy, peace, longsuffering, kindness, goodness, faithfulness, gentleness, self-control. Against such there is no law".*

(Galatians 5:22–23, NKJV)

---

7   vocabulary.com, Inc., a division of IXL Learning, 2023.

Chapter 11

———— ⚭ ————

You Are Not Fighting Against Flesh and Blood...

Do not be fooled by the author of confusion.

As I spoke with the Wise Men and godly friends, I began to see the error in our ways. I saw the work of the enemy unravel. I normally would have been keenly aware of the errors and the enemy. However, since I was wandering around in the dark valley, I no longer had the ability to see or hear. I was navigating in treacherous territory blind and alone, growing weaker the longer I strayed.

We were unhealthy, and our marriage was a toxic wasteland. The enemy and his troops must have had a field day in our home. Perhaps we were a challenge in the beginning. Soon becoming less appealing to the enemy, we were easy. The weakest member of the enemy camp could be assigned to us. Once the strategy of darkness was set in motion, we kept the flame ignited.

Failing to recognize our issues at or near onset brought disappointment. I believe being continually subjected to the behavior desensitized me, finally becoming our new normal. No longer discerning what was right and godly. Behaviors that were previously forbidden were tolerable. Had someone conducted themselves in this manner in the past, they would not have remained in my life.

I considered my ways, noting my image was distorted and sickly. Honestly, I wouldn't have remained married to myself. I no longer handled conflict or disagreements with respect. I operated with an agenda to win arguments. I spoke over and interrupted my husband. I didn't cuss when I met Brennan. Now, I immediately started using profanity when we had a disagreement.

I was working one day and heard the word "spit scream." I asked what it meant. They began to describe it as someone who was angry and screaming. They explained it was so loud that spit flew out of their mouth when they screamed. Suddenly, a light bulb came on, followed by a wave of sadness. I knew exactly what they meant. I had experienced and saw firsthand what a spit scream was. My husband had screamed at me this forceful and spit flew.

One day, the Holy Spirit gave me a vision of Brennan and me. It opened my eyes to a different perspective. In the image, there were two huge whitetail bucks fighting one another. The bucks rammed and locked horns, fighting for victory. They obtained abrasions and lacerations as they brushed up against trees, thorn bushes, and barbed wire. The Bucks were so focused on winning they weren't aware of the damage occurring. Eventually, they fought until both collapsed onto the ground; exhaustion had set in. Even then, they still fought, laying down as spurts of energy came. Eventually, one buck expired, and the other barely hung on to life. The surviving buck was doomed for death as he lay prisoner to the dead buck's horn lock.

After thinking about this vision, I was surprised because I was a buck instead of a doe. I realized I was overstepping my boundaries in areas of the marriage. I was not a submissive wife. I was not exhibiting the fruit of the spirit. I was not choosing to show God's kind of love.

I was saddened because that was a perfect illustration of us. I've seen those types of buck fights on videos. The bucks have tunnel vision, and nothing seems to distract them. That was how I felt when we fought, exhausted physically and mentally. We were so caught up in winning that we, directly and indirectly, damaged one another. So, like the bucks, was the victory really a victory?

You can only serve one master at a time. When you do good works, you serve your Father God. When you do evil, your father is Satan. This is a reminder no matter what life throws at you, there is always a choice in how you react. If you do not stay alert, then you will fight the wrong battles.

I don't know who my audience is. We come from different backgrounds and beliefs, even if we attend the same church. In saying that, I believe we battle what is unseen more often than what we see. It's not always easy to detect the sources of opposition, especially in the heat of the moment. Every outburst of anger is not demonic, but it's worth a second thought. You could be dealing with someone who just lost a job, isn't feeling well, or received bad news.

Have you ever been in a situation, and after reflecting, you knew it was deeper than you thought? I am sharing a few incidents that occurred, and I knew it was different. I knew I wasn't dealing with flesh and blood. There was more going on than I understood at that given time. The enemy was at work, and I was not at war with Brennan.

For we wrestle not against flesh and blood, but against principalities, against powers, against the rulers of the darkness of this world, against spiritual wickedness in high places.

Ephesians 6:12 (KJV)

These are more obvious acts. I knew immediately my husband was like the enemy. Brennan demonstrated harsh words and behavior against God. Brennan mocked God much like he mocked me. I wanted to run and hide. I had difficulty comprehending how a Christian could be so bold and deliberate against God. His actions were so absurd it would cause me to take a few steps away. I felt lightning was going to strike him at any moment.

My husband purposely said the curse word I didn't tolerate, which is "GD." When he was mad at me, he said it multiple times in a row with a sinister look. A lady shared a great point with me about cursing God. She said Satan hates God and often uses the mouths of others to curse Him. Dr. Adrian Rogers elaborated on the third commandment in his message, The Name Above All Names. Dr. Rogers warned about taking the Lord's name in vain. Dr. Rogers explained this was an insult flung into the face of God. Dr. Rogers didn't condone the following behaviors but provided a sin comparison. He said the thief gets property or the murderer gets revenge. When someone takes the Lord's name in vain, they only get judgment.

I recall the first event that opened my eyes to the work of the enemy. This occurred earlier in our marriage, and I was taken aback when it happened. I urgently wanted wisdom and guidance on it. I set up an appointment with one of the Wise Men, The Truth Bearer. The incident began with Brennan and I arguing in our master bathroom. He paced in and out from our master bedroom; there is no door between the rooms. The argument was unproductive, and nothing was being accomplished. Something felt different in the way he acted. I'm not sure if it was Brennan's word or deeds. Perhaps it was the hostility that alerted me.

I recalled an entry in a Sean Bolz book[8] when, in spiritual warfare, we don't act weird. We do what Jesus would do. I remembered what Jesus said to Peter in Matthew 16:23: "Get the behind me, Satan." I silently said it towards my husband, adding, "In Jesus' name, amen." I said it quietly under my breath because it was not intended for fleshly ears. I no longer got the words out, and there was silence.

---

8   *Prophecies, Prayers & Declarations Breakthrough*, Sean Bolz.

I waited for a moment because I thought Brennan was distracted by his phone. I looked behind and around me in the bathroom, but there was no sign of Brennan. I went into the master bedroom, living area, kitchen, no sign of Brennan. I went outside, and Brennan drove away from the house. I can't explain how fast he had to move. From the moment I said that verse to the moment he drove away, it seemed like lightspeed. I am certain whatever was battling me knew who I belonged to at that moment. It knew I understood my authority through Jesus and awareness to use His Word. The Wise Man Truth Bearer prayed with me about this incident, and I received God's peace.

Another thing I can't explain occurred in the middle of the night. I am a sound sleeper. It takes vigorous shaking or a loud noise to awaken me. One night, I was sleeping soundly, and I was awakened by something. I only saw darkness, and Brennan was asleep. I dozed off for a moment, and I felt it again but saw nobody. It felt annoying, yet there was nothing. It felt like the irritation or annoyance I experienced as a kid, when the neighborhood boys picked on me. I couldn't see anything, but I felt a heavy, annoying presence (plural). It was above me (between my bed and the wall), near the ceiling. It felt deliberate; it wanted me to be scared, to feel unwelcome. It wanted me to leave. I was so sleepy, and maybe this was lazy. I had a calm and protected feeling and said, "Leave, in the name of Jesus, amen." The presence went away, and I went to sleep. I didn't go on without wondering what that was. Another reminder: we do not fight against flesh and blood but against principalities and powers.

I am disappointed with myself about the next events. They deserved a more thorough response, and one might describe it as negligence. I felt like I was not deserving to be called a mom. I recognized the work of the enemy but let it go. I knew the enemy target has always been to destroy families. "If you pierce the family, you pierce its society" (Dr. Del Tackett). I didn't become like the protective grizzly bear with cubs; going into spiritual warfare, I knew better.

I mothered my sons to the best of my ability. Of course, more thought and maturity accompanied the last child. I was extremely structured with Kale's evening routine. After his bath, we read a book of his choice, then the Bible. We read a short children's devotional, we both participated in our gratitude journal and ended with prayer. This sounds like a lot, but it didn't take long. He knew it was bedtime at the end, so I didn't wrestle with him about going to bed like I did with his brother, KZ.

Shortly after I married my husband, this nightly routine slowly dissipated. Until finally, we no longer had a routine. I felt miserable because Kale looked forward to the nightly routine. I placed our used movie tickets, sporting event tickets, or any activity ticket inside the gratitude journal. Kale would occasionally go to the journal and reminisce about our life events. Of all the failures, in my current situation, this one carried the most weight. The shame was plaguing, no matter how hard I worked to conceal it, it kept surfacing.

Early in our marriage, our mealtimes became awkward. I was on pins and needles at the bar where we ate. Brennan berated me for not teaching my thirteen-year-old son better table manners. My son stabbed a meatball with a fork and ate it like a corndog. I honestly never noticed, and I immediately corrected my son because he needed to know proper manners. It wasn't long until Brennan found another issue with my son. He started complaining because my son didn't cut the bites small enough. Brennan said my son couldn't help it because he wasn't taught any better, which caused me to feel like a horrible mother. I was uneasy, thereafter, waiting for Brennan to criticize him.

One night, we were eating at the kitchen bar. Brennan was on my right, and my son was on the left. During the meal, I noticed Brennan wasn't eating. He sat with his arms folded over his chest. I looked at his face, seeing the most malevolent glares I'd ever seen on a human face. I briefly worried about what he was mad at. I realized he wasn't looking at me, and it appeared he was glaring at my son.

I looked to my left, and my son was eating with his head hung low. He faced downwards, looking towards his lap. His eyes barely peeked up over the top of his glasses. He placed food into his mouth and looked down as he chewed and swallowed his food. It was like he appeared to feel unwelcome and inferior. It reminded me of a time I fed a stray dog, how it would ease up to the food, keeping his eyes down.

I looked back to my right, and Brennan was still glaring at my son. I looked back to my left, and my son was still fixed in a low posture. I whipped my attention back to Brennan. I can only imagine my facial expression as I became enraged. I sternly and loudly asked Brennan, "What are you looking at?" Brennan immediately snapped out of the glare, directing his attention to me. Brennan looked surprised as his normal face returned. I sternly asked again, "What are you looking at?" Brennan shrugged and had a totally different demeanor. Brennan asked me what was wrong. He had no idea what he looked like and that he had been glaring. Later that evening, I asked my son if he felt okay at dinner and if anything bothered him. He told me it was fine, and he didn't notice anything. I don't think either one of them knew what was going on. There was an uninvited guest at our dinner. It was the enemy behind the skin and bones.

I hated the feeling I experienced each time we sat at the table. I knew quietly my husband was noting everything that wasn't up to his standard. Brennan would not immediately share his findings but held until the next dispute. I remembered something that shut Brennan down in all arguments. Any reference from The Bible would instantly create silence. My knowledge wasn't vast, but I had a foundation, and it was enough. At some point, I remembered the impact of bringing up God's Word.

I knew it was imperative to introduce the Word during dinner. I decided to bring Kale's bedtime routine to the dinner table. Each day, I read a devotion or scripture and summarized it. I brought my summary to dinner along with the gratitude journal. I shared what I learned while we ate. Then, I asked my son and Brennan to tell me something they were grateful for. I saw the tide turn immediately, and dinner soon became a breath of fresh air. I was reprimanded for not teaching my son real-life matters. I also noted my husband was not a thankful person. My husband had difficulty thinking of something he was thankful for. He provided answers comparable to the answers my son provided at six to seven years old. The things he mentioned were silly, like, "My wife's staring crow face." The environment at the dinner table changed from intimidation and fear to life and victory! For God has not given us a spirit of fear, but of power and of love and of a sound mind (2 Timothy 1:7).

On another occasion, we were having a heated argument in our bedroom. It got to a point where I was commanded to get out and give the wedding ring back. It was earlier in our marriage, and I complied. Brennan insisted we go upstairs and tell the kids and leave the bedroom. I thought it was odd but followed him out of the bedroom. Something about the direction of this argument felt different. I felt the target had shifted, and it was unusual to leave our bedroom. I hurried to catch him as he went through the kitchen and up the stairs. He went straight to my son's room, flinging open his door. My son's eyes widened, and he looked surprised as Brennan rushed in. My son was standing between his bed and his bathroom door as Brennan approached him. Brennan harshly told my son that he and I would be moving out. My son is very laid back and quiet. He quietly listened as Brennan continued complaining. My son finally said okay and then asked, "Are you done?" Brennan escalated at his response and began yelling towards my son, "This is my house, and you and your mom are going to get out!" My son and I looked at Brennan, and he finally stormed out of my son's bedroom.

Brennan was going to bypass his son's bedroom. I said, "Oh no, we need to let your son know too!" Brennan didn't want to tell his son. I felt he must know it was disrespectful and outlandish behavior.

Perhaps he didn't want to subject his son to the conduct. After I reflected on that event much later, I realized it was bullying and intimidating behavior. Failing to respond properly was negligent on my end. I had a responsibility to protect my son; no action sent a message, I allowed it.

Another example of dealing with the unseen realm involved an experience with dogs. I feel dogs have a higher sense of awareness. The story of Balaam and his donkey surfaced recently, reminding me of this experience. The story comes from Numbers 22:21–41. I believe it confirmed, at least to me, that something supernatural happened. In summary, Balaam's donkey disobeyed him when he quit walking. The Lord gave the donkey the ability to speak to Balaam. The donkey asked Balaam why he got beaten. The Lord opened Balaam's eyes, and he saw the angel of the Lord with sword drawn. Balaam would have been killed, and the donkey spared had it continued walking.

I share my dog's story because I believe the dogs sensed something. I can't explain what happened. Maybe one day I will find out.

The beagle is one of the most vocal dog breeds, and he can make three different sounds: a standard bark, a yodel-like sound called a bay (which he uses when hunting), and a howl.

This story occurred during my health crisis, discussed in Chapter 1. It was a very cold day, and my first husband was very ill. He had a doctor's appointment that day and asked me to tend to his beagles. The kennels were outdoors, covered, and on a concrete slab. The kennels were approximately 150 yards from the fence where we parked. As soon as you exited your vehicle, the beagles were loudly baying and bouncing around. They knew it was mealtime.

They excitedly jumped and bayed constantly while you cleaned the kennels. They seemed to get louder as you scooped poop and washed the floor with the water hose. The beagles only stopped baying when you dumped the food in their bowls. I was bundled up in Carhartt overalls and had finished scooping poop and was wrangling the water hose when a cardiac episode hit me suddenly.

I was going down fast and felt impending doom. I didn't have a phone, and I didn't have the air to make it to the house. I stood still, tried breathing techniques, and sat down on the ground. Nothing helped; I was running out of air, and my heart felt like it was going to explode.

The beagles bayed louder as I would have normally started feeding them by now. In the snap of your fingers, in synchronized timing, all the beagles stopped baying. At the exact same time, they went into their dog houses. They never stopped baying, not once, unless they had food in their bowls.

I moved into a lying position on the cold ground, seeing tunnel vision. I felt like I was going to pass out or even die, wondering how long it would be before I was discovered. As I lay flat for a few moments, my heart rate began to slow down. My shortness of breath started to diminish. I took a few slow, deep breaths, realized I might live, and got up on my knees.

In synchronized timing, the beagles came out of their dog houses. They all started baying and bouncing around again. It was the weirdest thing I'd ever witnessed. I was more curious about what just happened with the beagles than the heart episode. The oddity of the beagle's behavior and the fact that it was synchronized in perfect timing blew me away. While I was in distress, the beagle's strange behavior caused me to look around. I sensed something was happening around me, but there was nothing seen or heard. I have no confirmation of what happened, but I believe it was significant, perhaps an unseen battle.

I recall these incidents so that you reflect on your own life. We aren't always dealing with skin and bones; sometimes, it's deeper. In my circumstances, I focused on flesh and blood, and I suffered greater and longer instead of fighting the source of the problems (enemy).

Stay alert! Watch out for your great enemy, the devil. He prowls around like a roaring lion, looking for someone to devour.

1 Peter 5:8 (NLT)

The Fisherman

The perfect fishing day was now a full-fledged battle. We learned the fisherman acted promptly and made the wise choice to seek medical attention.

There is more to be considered than the single decision to seek medical care. Deciding to seek medical care was a step in the right direction, but more is required. The fisherman had to choose to put his faith in and surrender to the medical professionals. A patient can present to a hospital, but they may become non-compliant at any moment. The required medical treatment can be irritating, painful, and frustrating as you trust in the medical team. Sometimes, the patient may experience additional pain or suffering from the injury as it reaches its damage potential. Certain medical treatments and plans are painful but necessary.

The fisherman once surrendered with his full faith placed in the professionals, would only be required to comply and trust. The fisherman would regress at any point if he stopped trusting and became non-compliant. The fisherman's body could react in unexpected ways during the recovery and healing process. His continual awareness and adherence to the treatment plan were imperative. The fisherman required extensive care and attention, but he had minimal lasting effects from the toxic venom. The fisherman lived to tell his story of survival.

Chapter 12

———∞———

Pity Parties, Hate Trains, and Grief Gutters

Once home and alone, despite the Wise Men's impartation of wisdom and truth, staying focused was difficult. I was being guided out of the pit, and scales were being removed from my eyes. The temptation to look back on the past was intense. I thought, after moving, life would get better, but it got worse. I dreaded coming home each day after work. My life seemed to no longer have value. I never felt suicidal but felt like I had no purpose on earth and was of no use to anyone. Each time I reflected on my failures, disappointment covered me like a weighted blanket. The weighted blanket grew heavier the longer I reflected. I recalled from my health healing the importance of being thankful and praising God. Being thankful in the pit reminded me of the abounding blessings when things looked grim. However, on my worst days, it was not easy to shake the vast number of emotions I felt.

A visit with one of the Wise men surprised me when we discussed my coping mechanisms. She, in a matter-of-fact tone, said, "Your pushing things aside isn't working now, is it?" I was taken aback for a moment. Then, admitted my coping method was not working. My attempt to field trauma and pain only got me so far in life. Now, I was out of my league in this type of suffering. I was thankful this cup of suffering wasn't served to me until I was in my forties.

My heart began to break for people. Those experiencing trauma and suffering early in their life. I wondered how the damage affected them in the long term. I wondered if I would deal with my issues forever or if they would slowly go away. I wondered what kind of person I would be on the other side.

All I hoped for was that Brennan would acknowledge his part, be remorseful, and repent. Someone once said repentance produces change, whereas remorse merely produces sorrow. I longed for the day we would come together and work through it. Multiple times after moving out and into the second location, I was infused with optimism. My husband pitched the idea of seriously working on our marriage, but it was always short-lived. We would be so loving and caring, expressing how much we missed one another. Soon after, our issues surfaced in conversation, then spiraled out of control, finally crashing.

I was so heartbroken, having no idea how miserable this condition could make you feel. I could only think about Brennan. I would have the grandest of pity parties. Not only daily but multiple parties' minutes and hours apart. My mind cycled through my husband's over-the-top love. Everywhere I looked, there was something that reminded me of Brennan.

We did everything together, from cooking meals, chores, errands, work, and relaxing. I had a gigantic void in my life. Even though we grew older daily, our hearts became younger. We were childlike in many aspects; laughter and playfulness were common in the reconciliation and calm phase. We joked and picked at one another continuously. I recalled the time we went to Mexico for a quick getaway. We decided to get massages beachside in a massage tent. We both had our faces covered with a cloth to filter out the sunlight. At the point I thought the massage was ending, it quickly began. The massager ran two hands high upon my thigh. The hands were so high on my thigh that it caused me to sit up. I sat up instantly, swinging a towel, trying to hit whoever was there. And to my surprise, Brennan had quietly switched places with my massage therapist, playing a trick on me.

Brennan was a cuddler, and I loved that. He held me close while we watched movies. I loved to smell Brennan as we cuddled. He and I fit together perfectly, like two adjoining pieces of a jigsaw puzzle. I never napped in my life except during pregnancy. I could cuddle with Brennan and be napping within a matter of minutes. Brennan made me feel comfortable when we were getting along. He went out of his way to make me feel special.

So, after I ran through all the amazing things, then the pity party began. The pity party caused me to focus on the "what was." Ensnaring me with hurts from the past and present. Multiple times a day, I went from sobbing to anger, boarding the hate train. I left the pity party and boarded the hate train heading to Uglyville. Some days, I'd be in Uglyville so long I'd find myself back to the beginning of our marriage. The hate train conductor was a great historian. The train conductor took me to all the hiding spots where my hurts were buried in Uglyville.

Remaining in the pity party and hate train cycle was harmful. I couldn't figure out how to get over this or out of the repetitive cycle. One of my attempts to get out of the cycle was to focus on the ugliness. I hoped it would cause me to want nothing to do with Brennan. That would work for a moment, but it didn't work long and kept me feeling angry.

Lo and behold, another unhealthy phase crept into the cycle. First, it was the pity party, the hate train, now wallowing in the grief gutter. In the grief gutter, I recall everything I had lost, going into fits of despair. In the grief gutter, I lost track of time and purpose. I looked around, seeing the evidence of loss. The only thing that remained in my life from the past is a Christmas tree and family photos. Each night before I went to sleep, I flipped my pillow because one side was tear-soaked. I went to sleep sobbing with wet, tear-filled Kleenex tissue all around me. I woke up each morning with red, puffy eyes. I scanned the strange room as my eyes adjusted to the daylight. Pondering for a moment, asking where I was. It was several months before I stopped waking up, wondering if this was really happening or a dream.

I seemed to take everyday situations and make them worse than what was actual. An example was when I got COVID that winter. My son stayed with his dad while I recovered. I had mild to moderate symptoms and was very thankful for mild symptoms. Even though I was thankful, here came negative thinking. I thought how horrible it was that no one would be by to check on me. Then I thought if I were to die of complications, no one would know for days. I was suddenly saddened by a morbid image of me inside my house, dead, possibly for days. Kale texted me every day while I was sick. He asked me how I was doing, and I remember thinking how thoughtful he was. Kale had no idea how much his daily texts touched my soul and lifted me. I believe that was God's love being shared through my son. God loves us, and he wanted me to know I wasn't forgotten.

I remember being so eager to find relief but didn't know what to pray. I looked back at my journal entries, noting multiple times I wrote "help" and "I trust You." I didn't know what else to say to God. I trusted and knew the Lord would get me through this because I walked through healing. I couldn't figure out how He would rescue me from this type of pit.

One night, I remember being so desperate and stupid that I foolishly asked God for help, adding, even if it's Your *tough love*. Deep down, I sensed I needed a spiritual slap in my face. I felt myself falling to pieces. I believe not having anyone to talk to made things worse. I had no one to vent to or ask for advice. I feel that sometimes worldly advice is better than leaning on your feelings or talking to yourself.

Shortly after my idiotic request, I got a word, and boy, it was tough love! I do not recommend asking for tough love. Instead, I pray you recall what you've been taught, unlike me. This is what I heard the Lord say after I asked for His tough love, "When you left Me, did you cry and weep? Did you lose all concentration and focus?" I was immediately mortified. I knew I didn't miss a beat when I ventured away from my relationship with God.

I felt like a dirty, rotten scoundrel. I didn't feel a thing when I walked away from my relationship with the Lord. I turned all my attention and focus to Brennan some years ago. I also went to the extreme in relationship recovery efforts with Brennan and none to God. I spent hours reading scriptures and articles about marriage. I sought and attended counseling for my marriage. I have no recovery efforts to speak of in my relationship with God.

That discovery of my lack of God was sobering. I soon found myself going deeper in thought. I wondered how many people turn from Jesus each day. Here I am, about to lose it over one person who has deliberately turned from me, yet Jesus experiences this often. There is no telling how often that occurs, and Jesus still loves us the same. This embarrassing tidbit of tough love became a tool I used going forward. I used the tool when I found myself about to have a pity party, board the hate train, or slide into the grief gutter.

From out of the stores of my memory banks, I remembered a teaching about idols from the late Adrian Rogers. It had been several years since I heard it, but it appeared out of thin air. Funny thing, as I was writing this portion of the testimony, I heard the message yesterday. The message is called People God Uses. One of the qualities was explained from the story of Gideon in Judges 6–7. God used cleansed people who had no idols in their lives and were surrendered. This was the part I remembered, so loud and clear. Adrian Rogers said, "An idol is anything you love, fear, serve, or value more than God."

This shook me to the core. I immediately realized I had idols in my life. I felt my tears dry up and my sorrows and woe-is-me go into a corner and hide. To have idols in my life was to break the first and great commandment, "Thou shalt love thy Lord God with all thy heart, and all thy soul, and with all thy mind." I had idols in my life, and the constant attention and focus on these idols removed God from number 1.

I understood, from the lesson years ago, that idols were things like work, money, sex, or drugs. Now I understand an idol is anything you love, fear, serve, or value more than God. I was giving excessive time and attention to my emotions. I continually kept Brennan, my circumstances, and suffering my primary focus. In doing so, I loved, valued, and served myself more than God. I loved my husband more than God. I feared the unknown and further loss more than I feared God. Self-focus edged its way into becoming my issue. Someone once said, "Self-focus is quiet pride."

I was blown away at the thought of it all when I put it into perspective. I walked away from my relationship with God and replaced Him with idols. My oldest son described a very forceful punch as a haymaker. I believe if there was a haymaker (spiritual) slap, this was it. I experienced tremendous loss, pain, and suffering. I had valid reasons to be in the sea of emotions. I believe it is healthy to cry and get it all out. However, the problem was the constant pity parties, hate train rides, and wallowing in the grief gutter. Refusal to move on and self-soothe was forming idols. This revelation wasn't a quick fix. Perhaps it's best described as my attitude adjuster. It caused me to dry it up (quit crying) as soon as I was headed to the pity party, hate train, or grief gutter.

Currently, as I write, I continue to get revelation and lessons from my story. Sunday at Church, Pastor Jacob's message was titled "All of You." During the message, he spoke about what happens when you "white knuckle" something. This means whatever you are holding onto for dear life, you will lose it. We should be focused on Jesus, not anything else. I was convicted and remembered I had Brennan/marriage white-knuckled and wouldn't let go. I lost focus on all things except that, and I lost Brennan/marriage. Let me clarify: The Lord doesn't want your marriages to fail. We are to focus on God first. It's disgraceful to know the effort I put into something and only minimal towards God, who gave His Son for us.

For God so loved the world, that he gave his only begotten Son, that whosoever believeth in him should not perish, but have everlasting life.

John 3:16 (NIV)

Chapter 13

---∞---

Dude, Where's My Car?

This chapter is named after a movie. I don't know if I ever watched it. I do know I said these exact words during my next discovery. It occurred a little over a year after I relocated. This was not a chapter in my book. After the events unfolded, I felt it created finality in my situation, crossing the Rubicon.

It was a cold Friday in November, nearing the Thanksgiving holiday. I was scheduled to leave early because my son had routine appointments. This was a rushed Friday because my son was eager to participate in a family tradition. He was going to Happy Hollow, the family deer camp. The men in his dad's family camp there the week of Thanksgiving. I got pushback for keeping the scheduled appointments because it was the opening day of cabin week.

Around 2:00 p.m., I gathered my things and headed out into the cold. I bundled up and started the long walk to the back of the parking lot. I noticed the semitrailer was still in the parking lot, in front of my row of parking. I continued to walk, looking at the area where my car should have been, but I couldn't see it. I began thinking

I must have parked further behind the semi than I realized. As I got closer, I still didn't spot my vehicle. I leaned my body to see further around the semitrailer. I did not see my vehicle, and I was almost to the spot where I parked; it was not there. I stopped walking and briefly ran through the morning, recalling exactly where I parked.

If there was a feeling that struck me when I realized my vehicle was gone, it was helplessness. I was forty-five miles from home, stranded and powerless. I quickly thought of the possibilities of what happened to my vehicle. I thought of two options, one being the company moved my vehicle; perhaps it was in the way of the semi. The other option was Brennan. I shook my head, turned around, and started walking back to the building. I asked myself, *Dude, where's my car?* I wondered if Brennan was hidden in the parking lot, watching his evil plan unfold. I gave him the benefit of the doubt, hoping he wouldn't sink to this level.

I calmly walked back towards the building. I thought of any other possibilities and eliminated my company from the list. The company would have notified me if they needed me to move my vehicle. I had both vehicle keys, and I wondered how Brennan accessed my vehicle. I thought he may have called a wrecker. He could have had another key fob made because both of our names are on the title, joined by the word "and." I went back into my department and straight to my manager's office. By this time, rage engulfed me. I asked her to call security, explaining my vehicle was missing. Security didn't answer, and she walked me down to the security suite.

I notified security of my findings. They asked me to walk outside and show them the exact parking spot. They needed the exact location for the surveillance review. I showed him where I parked my vehicle, and we walked back inside. I was asked to write a statement about the incident. I asked my manager to send a co-worker to help me as I walked through this situation. Security hesitantly asked if a debt collector could have taken the vehicle. I said no, it was not a possibility. They also asked who was on the title and who had keys. Security notified tribal police so a case could be created for a missing vehicle. Tribal police were going to be a little while. Security said I could go back to my office while I waited. I decided to go back upstairs, and I went to Aleisha's office (my director). I needed to hear God's truth in this situation, and I knew Aleisha would deliver it. I was in a rage and very hurt, realizing the only person who could have taken the vehicle was Brennan.

I entered Aleisha's office and broke down as I told her what happened. She immediately started to encourage me. Then, as I expressed my anger and how I wished to react, she corrected me. My co-worker was still with me and had many years of law enforcement experience. He provided legal advice and what not to do, as I shared my plan to get the car back. I knew I was in a safe space and the conversation would be kept confidential, so I vented. Aleisha said, "Ashley, it's just a car!" I explained that I didn't necessarily care about the car; it was the act that angered me, and I felt violated.

Aleisha didn't know why this angered me. I summarized it to her, but this is a more detailed account. The year prior, Brennan said he faced financial challenges multiple times. I felt sorry for him and offered to help make the hefty payment. I didn't want to because it was over a thousand dollars a month. I no longer made the same pay compared to the last fifteen to twenty years. Brennan often reminded me of what a luxurious gift this vehicle was. He expressed I should be more appreciative because no one had ever paid for my vehicles. Now, I asked myself if this was really a gift. If so, what a lousy gift. Along with the hefty payment, the insurance was very expensive. The vehicle's financial burden grew as it required premium gas and high-performance tires.

After I accepted the vehicle burdens, another burden was placed on me. My husband was adamant about being added to my health, dental, and vision insurance. I wasn't going to because it was after the divorce was filed. I wasn't obligated to add him to my plan. I felt sorry for Brennan and added him and his son. The monthly cost of my health insurance plan increased by a couple of hundred dollars. I didn't share this last part with my director and coworker. I reflected on our lifestyles since the drug bust and relocation. I expressed to my husband how tough it was going to be with the additional debts. My husband seemed to be okay with the struggle being shifted to me. I saw how drastically my life changed, and my husband appeared to be the same or better. He didn't work and enjoyed the retired life; this was the root of my anger.

Aleisha spoke the truth about the situation and prayed over me. She said something that provided a better perspective to look from. Aleisha suggested I thank Brennan for taking my car. When she said that I immediately perked up. I thought, you're right! I will no longer have a steep vehicle payment, insurance, premium gas, and high-performance tires. I needed two tires at that time, and the tires were only rated for 12,000 to 14,000 miles. I commute now, and the savings in tires would be a relief.

Tribal police arrived shortly after and created a case file and finished the process. I reached out to the vehicle manufacturer, and they were able to locate my vehicle. They would not disclose the location to me because this was a civil matter. The officer received the location but wouldn't share it due to liability reasons. The tribal officer shared the vehicle was local. They would send out a third party to try to retrieve my personal property. As the process was coming to an end, the officer asked if I wanted to call my husband. The officer thought he might cooperate. I attempted to call him, but he didn't answer, and it went to voicemail. Later that evening, the officer followed up, saying they were not able to reach Brennan. The officer confirmed he was in possession of the vehicle. I explained he watched his place like a hawk. He screens all his visitors with security cameras, I doubted he would answer.

I deliberated about the events on that cold November day. I asked myself, *Who comes to a woman's workplace and steals her vehicle?* My first thought was, *Well, Brennan took your vehicle for a month. Are you really shocked?* I say steal because he took it without notification or warning. His plan was premeditated and intentional. He surreptitiously stole my vehicle like a thief in the night. I considered his act to be lower than a common thief. The common thief doesn't necessarily know who he steals from. My husband knew his victims: a single mom with a minor child. My husband knew my situation and made his decisions. I speculated on who the accomplices were; this was at least a two-man job. I felt it was for the best if I didn't know who participated in this act.

Brennan stole from a working mom who works full time to support a family. The working mom was currently providing full health benefits for the thief and the thief's son. The thief didn't only steal from the woman, but he stole from her child. I can only think of one word to describe this heinous act: cruel. The thief may have had a right to the vehicle. However, the property and possessions inside the vehicle didn't belong to him. My husband made no attempts to reach out to me or return my property. I was in constant contact with my attorney, urging her to help me get my property back.

The timing of this violation couldn't have been more calculated. I was beginning to heal, move forward, and focus on my relationship with God. I knew the enemy wanted to inflict pain on me because I was moving closer to my heavenly Father. I was deeply hurt and became angry when nothing happened to Brennan. Not only did he steal the vehicle, but he was driving it around. It appeared arrogant and condescending. Imagine someone coming into your home stealing from you. Later, you see them publicly strutting around, consequence-free. They are donning your stolen clothing, jewelry, and apparel. It felt like Brennan was flashing a trophy around, wanting all to see because there were no consequences.

I cried about it but knew I couldn't stay in that place long. I redirected my hurt to a promise from God's word, knowing God would fight my battle. I was informed I could steal my vehicle back. If my husband parked it in a public setting, I could legally drive it away. I highly considered it and other possible pranks. I, not in my own strength, exercised great self-control when the opportunities were presented.

To all who mentioned my legal right to steal it back, I explained we were better than that. I was reminded of David in 1 Samuel chapter 24. David restrained himself and his men from killing Saul when the opportunity presented. Instead, David secretly cut off a corner of Saul's robe. David hadn't wronged Saul, yet Saul wanted to destroy him. The lesson is to treat others with kindness regardless of how they treat us. First Samuel 24:13 (KJV) says, "As saith the proverb of the ancients, Wickedness proceedeth from the wicked: but mine hand shall not be upon thee."

I heard a message the weekend after this happened. It spoke volumes to me in this very situation. The message was from Acts chapter 28, and Pastor Robert Madu at Social Dallas titled the message "Make It Make Sense." In the message, he focused on Paul being shipwrecked on the island of Malta. Pastor Madu said our Malta is somewhere you didn't plan on being. In Malta, all the pieces of the shipwreck are surrounding you.

In the message, one of the points Pastor Madu made was the pieces of our wreckage have purpose for someone else. My vehicle and property within were stolen, and I had pieces scattered around. I knew, at that moment, that my unfortunate circumstance had a purpose. The other thing that stuck out was when Pastor Madu shared about Paul being bitten by a poisonous viper snake. Paul was bitten after they were safe on the land. Pastor Madu shared out of Acts 28:3 about how the snake latched or fastened itself to Paul's hand and wouldn't let go. Pastor Madu explained a snake doesn't usually do that. Pastor Madu believed it was a demonic attack on Paul. Paul was determined to complete his mission to fulfill God's purpose.

I reflected on that story, believing my wreckage had a purpose. Even if I can't see it now, I just know. I felt my husband's egregious act was the enemy biting and latching onto me. Hoping to cause me to stumble or fall into the pity party, hate train, and grief gutter cycle. I wanted to retaliate, I wanted to cry, I wanted to get even. I knew that wasn't the right way. Aleisha, so thankful for her, reminded me of a new song to sing called "Surrounded (Fight My Battles)" by Michael W. Smith. I sang this song over and over after the incident. I knew God was fighting for me. I also received a tidbit of revelation through a stewardship message. In the message, the preacher explained our things are not ours; they all belong to God. I instantly thought the vehicle and possessions weren't mine. The stolen property belonged to God. I felt God could handle this situation better than me.

Another helpful message from Pastor Robert Madu is called Get to the Good Part. Genesis 50:20 (NLT) says, "You intended to harm me, but God intended it all for good." Pastor Madu made a great point in this message about suffering. Pastor Madu explained suffering will produce something in you that good times never will! Pastor Madu reminded us of Romans chapter 5, that suffering produces perseverance, which builds character and produces hope.

I was able to see the purpose in one of my pieces shortly after this incident. I had extra money since my vehicle had been stolen. I heard and obeyed the Lord right after this happened when he said specifically who to share a monetary gift with. I found out afterwards the gift was forwarded, and a family who had been faithful and praying for a need was blessed. I wouldn't have had the extra money to share if it hadn't been for the broken pieces (stolen vehicle).

Something else happened because of this egregious act. It served a purpose; it caused me to continue down the right path. Since moving into the second location, I worried about what was right or wrong.

Constantly moving in and out of denial of my marital problems and relationship toxicity. I still stood in denial and disobedience (explained below) in the relational issues with Brennan. So much so, a few weeks before he stole the vehicle, we discussed working things out. I was preparing to move back in with Brennan at the end of the year.

He pitched a grand reconciliation process with a new beginning. Offering many promises with lots of changes. I agreed to participate in a rapid counseling regimen with my husband. Time was of the essence as the end of the year was nearing. I knew intense work was at hand if we were going to fix all the problems. I believed the counseling was going to resolve our problems, and Brennan could change.

Shortly after we started counseling, the relationship derailed. Then Brennan stole my vehicle, and something broke inside me that day. I don't know what it was about this act, but it finally tore me down. It was like switching on a light switch. The light shed insight on how deliberate and malicious this act was. I understood it was intended to inflict pain and suffering onto my son and me. It finally caused me to open my eyes. My husband had the freedom to choose; his spiteful choice affected me and others. No matter how hurtful, I knew God would use this for the greater good.

And we know that all things work together for good to them that love God, to them who are the called according to his purpose.

Romans 8:28 (KJV)

Above, the disobedience I mentioned was specific to our relationship. I must back up a little to the month before I relocated. I was still living with Brennan. The Holy Spirit gave me instruction to leave. In fact, it was like this: I was jogging after work, rounding the corner by our house to head north. As I rounded the corner, I felt a tap on my shoulder. As to signal me to turn my head around. I looked back over my shoulder, catching a glimpse of our house. The Holy Spirit said, "Run, don't look back."

I knew this meant marriage and circumstances making me sad. I teared up, but I said okay. I was filled with motivation to fulfill these words. I didn't understand and wondered if danger was on the horizon. I thought perhaps it was just a message to move on. I thought it was odd to hear "run" and then "don't look back." I immediately thought of Lot's wife in the Bible. She turned to ash, looking back, after the angel instructed them not to look back. Unfortunately, I was like Lot's wife and looked back often. I didn't look; I gawked. Subsequently, consequences occurred for looking back.

Another disobedient incident occurred after receiving an image at church. I received an image at church approximately four months after I relocated. Pastor Zach was speaking, and he ushered me into a position to receive the image. I saw myself as a little girl on a ledge with a boy (Brennan). On the ledge where he stood was a land full of darkness and death. I was picked up by Jesus, and He moved away from the ledge. There was a definitive separation of the lands. The one Jesus moved toward was green, lush, and sunny. The part that made me sad was when Jesus picked me up. I held Brennan's hand tightly even after Jesus picked me up. I heard the Lord say, "Come on, Ashley." I had to release Brennan's hand, feeling sorrow for him. I saw anguish in his face but felt I could no longer hold on (to us). I realized that I didn't have the ability to handle the situation. I understood I was with Jesus; that's where I needed to be. This image was a message to let go of Brennan and focus on my Lord and Savior. I released Brennan's hand but returned to him multiple times. I justified my actions by saying, "Perhaps that message was just release for a season." Deep inside, I knew that was not the truth.

Now I realize how patient God is with us (me specifically). I obeyed and fled the situation; however, I turned back numerous times. I placed hope into the wrong things. No person on earth would have extended that much patience. During this time, I recall how quickly I was judged for making poor decisions. I was judged for failing to meet their timelines in moving on and healing. They got frustrated easily and didn't take the time to understand. They lacked the capacity to know what I was dealing with at any given time. They didn't know poor choices stemmed from a lack of better options. I have a new appreciation for God's mercy and patience in my disobedience, ignorance, and distractedness. Patience, mercy, and listening to others will be something I extend more freely because He extended it to me. If you have been here, just know God's love hasn't changed for you, no matter how far off the path you are.

The LORD is longsuffering, and of great mercy, forgiving iniquity and transgression, and by no means clearing the guilty, visiting the iniquity of the fathers upon the children unto the third and fourth generation.

Numbers 14:18 (KJV)

Chapter 14

———— ∞ ————

The Paralyzed Man

Several days later, Jesus returned to Capernaum, and the news quickly spread that he was back in town. Soon there were so many people crowded inside the house to hear him that there was no more room, even outside the door. While Jesus was preaching the word of God, four men arrived, carrying a paralyzed man. But when they realized that they couldn't even get near him because of the crowd, they went up on top of the house and tore away the roof above Jesus' head. And when they had broken through, they lowered the paralyzed man on a stretcher right down in front of him! When Jesus saw the extent of their faith, he said to the paralyzed man, "My son, your sins are now forgiven."

Mark 2:1–5 (TPT)

This is one of the most important revelations I received as I climbed out of my pit. This verse crossed my path on social media. It was a meme with emphasis on your circle of friends. That is a great point: it is important who your friends are. I thought about the meme, chewing on it for a little while. Then, a light bulb moment, and I am forever changed.

Definition of Paralysis: Complete or partial loss of function, especially when involving the motion or sensation in a part of the body, loss of the ability to move, a state of powerlessness, or incapacity to act (Merriam-Webster, Inc., 2022).

The first revelation I received about this verse was pertaining to "the paralyzed man." I heard and read that scripture before and put little thought into it. I only viewed it as it was written he was physically paralyzed. My mind wandered into nurse thoughts, wishing they would've had wheelchairs back then. I wondered why he was paralyzed. I wondered if it was full paralysis. Then, I began to focus on the difficulties of the caretakers.

As I was thinking about the paralyzed man, boom, a question from the Holy Spirit. It was a two-part question, "Who is paralyzed? What paralyzes you?" I was dumbfounded for a minute. All of a sudden, I saw the paralyzed man differently. I realized those questions were for me. I asked myself if I was the paralyzed man. I began to assess and evaluate myself. I didn't have to think about it long.

I remember being paralyzed by fear during my health crisis. I was so fearful in the health crisis I didn't drive for a month. In my current situation, I lost the ability to move. I recalled being in a state of powerlessness. After the self-reflecting, I was clearly the paralyzed man on the mat. I was paralyzed by fear, confusion, trauma, disappointment, pain, heartache, and loss. I was so wrapped up (paralyzed) in the issues that I didn't know what to pray. I didn't know what to say to God or how to take the first step in healing. Now, the questions I had about the paralyzed man in Mark chapter

2, I asked of myself. I asked myself why I was paralyzed and what complications arose because of my state.

Paralysis (physical) cases vary in severity depending on the cause. There are different types of paralysis. A paralyzed patient may be able to perform some of the activities of daily living. Other patients are more severe, requiring twenty-four-hour care and support. I present a simple question pertaining to a person with more severe paralysis. What happens if they are left alone? For a short period, they may manage. Subsequently, a paralyzed patient, when left alone, will pass away. Due to the inability to provide the basic needs to survive.

I believe the same is true, in some respects, for an emotionally or mentally paralyzed person. That scripture is written for a purpose. For me, it revealed the importance of identifying what paralysis is in your life. I was paralyzed, and it worsened as more issues surfaced in the storm. I was oblivious to what was going on. I allowed my emotions to rule my days as I replayed each painful event over. Spiritually speaking, a once healthy and active woman started limping around, slowly losing mobility. Finally, I lost control of my limbs and only being able to drag myself around. In the darkness, my well-being grew sicker as I remained in this state.

In this paralyzed condition, I saw myself as a sheep, remembering messages about our Shepherd. The messages were from a podcast Mike Kai and Adrian Rogers audio message, "How to Get Right with God and Stay Right with God." Both of their messages were from Psalm 23. I wouldn't describe the messages as a feel-good lesson but one that convicted me. God's truth may convict you, but it's also a loving encouragement.

I recognized I was the stray and stubborn sheep. No matter what type, I was comforted because The Lord loves and protects all His sheep. I was disobedient, wanting my own way. Only to find myself lost and continually separated from the flock. The Lord used His staff to comfort me and to guide me. He gently used the crook of the staff to nudge me toward the right direction. However, I kept wandering and being disobedient.

As a sheep, I wandered into darkness, losing sight. I felt myself stuck in a dense thicket. I was immobile, unable to escape. The next step in shepherding seems brutal. But it's a life-saving measure for the disobedient sheep. The shepherd will use thy rod on the sheep and injure it. Yes, that sounds horrible, and you may ask what kind of God would do that to his sheep. The answer is a loving God. It is written in the Word:

Come and let us return to the Lord; For He has torn, but He will heal us; He has stricken, but He will bind us up.

Hosea 6:1 (NKJV)

The Lord uses the rod and injures the sheep; now, the sheep can't keep wandering away. The injured sheep must place all trust in the shepherd. The shepherd nurtures and cares for the sheep until it's healed. The Shepherd will nurse you back to health and carry you as you surrender to Him. As I rested and healed in the Sheperd's loving arms, thankfulness set in.

The Lord carried me until I was healthy enough to join the flock again. I am the only one to blame for my condition. I have always had the freedom to choose, and I made poor choices. I'm very thankful the Lord is patient and steadfast. Other shepherds would rather put a disobedient sheep out of its misery to tend to the obedient flock.

Adrian Rogers mentioned something, only understanding now, on this side of the valley. I see it as plain as day, but I couldn't see it in the darkness. Adrian Rogers shared the shepherd uses the crook to guide a straying mother sheep back towards her lamb. Adrian Rogers added if a mother sheep stays away from her lamb long enough, she will forget about the lamb. That was a gut-wrenching thought; I was headed to that state had it not been for the Shepherd intervening. I instantly thought about animals in nature. I remembered the sorrow I felt when a mother rejected her baby. I couldn't comprehend the rejection and what must be wrong with the mother. Nonetheless, there I was, at certain points, about to abandon my role as mom.

The chaos, trauma, heartache, and loss were overwhelming, causing me to lose focus of being a mom. My son was placed on the back burner. Each day, he went further down the list as I sifted through the pieces of the wreckage. Multiple times, when trying to reconcile things with Brennan, he convinced me to give up full custody of my son. He wanted me to choose him and put our marriage first, explaining moving away was the best option. He said my son could come with us, but my son wouldn't want to go. Shamefully, I was willing to give up full custody to salvage our marriage. No wonder the Shepherd leaves the ninety-nine and goes after the one. He knows what's at stake.

How think ye? If a man have an hundred sheep, and one of them be gone astray, doth he not leave the ninety and nine, and goeth into the mountains, and seeketh that which is gone astray? And if so be that he find it, verily I say unto you, he rejoiceth more of that sheep, than of the ninety and nine which went not astray. Even so it is not the will of your Father which is in heaven, that one of these little ones should perish.

Matthew 18:12–14 (KJV)

Back to the referenced scripture in Mark chapter 2, this is where the friend part came in. Another important focal point of the scripture, Mark 2:1–5, is the value of friends. What would have happened to the paralyzed man if there were no friends? He would've remained in his sick bed if it weren't for the friends or worse. Another light bulb moment occurred, and I arrived with two questions about friends. *What kind of friends do you have? What kind of friend are you?*

In my opinion, a person who reaches out in love is a friend. A friend is someone who makes you better. I don't primarily speak of long-time best friends or hang-out friends or vacation friends. It is the friend who extends God's kind of love to people they know and strangers. No conditions must be met because these types of friends love above all else.

This scripture further illustrates the friends I speak of.

> *"If you love those who love you, what credit is that to you?" Even sinners love those who love them. And if you do good to those who are good to you, what credit is that to you? Even sinners do that. And if you lend to those from whom you expect repayment, what credit is that to you? Even sinners lend to sinners expecting to be repaid in full. But love your enemies, do good to them, and lend to them without expecting to get anything back. Then your reward will be great, and you will be children of the Most High, because he is kind to the ungrateful and wicked. Be merciful, just as your Father is merciful.*

> Luke 6:32–36 (NIV)

This is embarrassing, but after some thought, I don't think I would be my own friend. I would be there initially, but I wasn't a steadfast friend. Steadfast, described one way, implies a steady and unwavering course in love, allegiance, or conviction in support. A steadfast friend is one who would remain diligent until the end. I don't believe I have been that kind of friend, and I don't think I'm alone.

I saw the lack of being a steadfast friend or family member in my nursing career. It was a frequent occurrence when I worked with the elderly and sick. My heart broke for my patients every time I witnessed the lack of steadfastness. It used to happen shortly after the diagnosis or loss of a family member.

People were usually quick to respond with texts, calls, and sending food. Family and friends came by for a visit and prayer but soon disappeared. While a patient endured a long battle, I witnessed the support slowly dissipate, then soon forgotten. It appeared to be human nature to lack steadfastness. Therefore, to find a person who sticks with you through suffering is a friend. So, this provided insight into my insufficiency and how to be better. I also identified who God sent to me as a friend throughout the darkness.

Chapter 15

———— ∞ ————

The Friends

Mark 2:1–5 referenced "the friends." There were four.

Hebrews 10:25 (KJV) says, "*Not forsaking the assembling of ourselves together, as the manner of some is; but exhorting one another: and so much the more, as ye see the day approaching.*"

Each friend demonstrated faith and obedience as they entered my darkness. They were equally important and instrumental in my rescue efforts. In God's rescue plan, He sent a friend at the perfect time. Each encounter ushered me a little further out of the darkness. They had no idea how much of an impact they had. Tokens of kindness, thoughtfulness, care, and compassion moved me little by little to the light.

These types of friends are very special and a rarity. In Mark chapter 2, it said the crowds were in the way inside and outside of the house. The crowds didn't stop the friends of the paralyzed man. Today, for example, the crowds might represent an actual crowd, our own life challenges, pains, limited time, lack of resources, sufferings, and other obstacles. The friends who helped in word, deed, or action placed their own needs and extra time aside to tend to me. The most valuable thing you can give someone is your time, whether it be seconds or minutes. You can't buy time, and it's meaningful to offer your time to others. It brings tears to my eyes when I think about the selfless acts and the impact each friend had on me.

The Lord saw my condition and knew it wasn't good for me to be alone. God would answer in the unlikeliest and most unexpected ways. I saw each friend as a light bearer. Each extension of love and support could be represented as grasping my mat. I was carried closer and closer to Jesus. Some of my friends held my mat longer than others, but it wasn't the time that was significant. It was the fact they held it at exactly the right time.

There were four friends in Mark 2:1–5 who carried the paralyzed man. I see four friends with the burden of my weight equally distributed among them so as not to overwhelm one friend. My friends carried me as I lay helpless and weak. When one friend completed their task, another stepped in. It was like a relay race, as God sent another friend, carefully transferring the baton (their grip on my mat). God placed each person's hand on my mat at the perfect time. Each one played a vital role in getting me to the roof and lowered down to Jesus. I hope as you read this, you realize you can shine a beautiful light into someone's darkness. You may be that friend whose hand is needed to hold a corner of the mat. You could be actively moving a paralyzed person a little closer to Jesus.

Some may try to disqualify themselves or feel they have nothing to contribute. Perhaps thinking it takes someone with more knowledge, money, or resources. Here is a fascinating tidbit: it only requires the simplest of acts. Back to the question, what happens to a paralyzed person if they are left alone? They will perish because their basic needs aren't met. Basic is the key word that equaled the simple things in my life. It's not the amount of time or what one did versus another. The important thing is they stepped out in faith and obedience, holding my mat.

Who were my friends? Who are your friends that you don't recognize?

Complete Strangers Were Friends

We didn't know each other, but they carried me a little further. These friends were good-hearted and sincere people. I just so happened to meet them during our daily routines. They had no idea how they impacted my day and changed my sadness into gladness.

Venturing out into the public seems so basic, but it caused uneasiness. My husband's criminal issues were aired on TV, creating unwanted attention. Brennan was well-known in the community. Going into public became a timed and strategic measure due to people's reactions to the news and rumors. I didn't notice until my husband pointed it out, but he was shunned by people in public places. So, the friendliness of complete strangers was so welcoming. Their kindness would be another hand on my mat.

Brennan requested the earliest hair appointment to avoid seeing people. Kale wasn't living with us, so I couldn't coordinate haircuts with Brennan. I heard about a popular barber in town but wasn't sure about using him. I assumed he knew about my husband and might be judgmental. My son and I decided to give him a try. I was overwhelmed at his acceptance and friendliness. Kale hated getting haircuts. He moaned and groaned about it for days leading up to it. Until we met Ryan Robertson. Ryan is a little older than my oldest son. He looks like a piece of art decorated with tattoos and his colorful taste in clothing. Ryan may be wearing a hat turned backwards or be rocking braids in his hair. Ryan takes his time with his clients and provides a superb service. But my son and I believe his personality was the best part of his service; he kept us entertained. He boosted our spirits at each visit. Ryan had no idea how much it lifted us out of the darkness. Ryan was the first person we conducted business with publicly. He made us feel welcome and like part of his family. It meant a lot to be treated with dignity and respect.

One day, I called AT&T about my phone service. The representative answered, saying hello, and asked how I was doing. I unexpectedly fell to pieces on the phone. My voice started quivering, and the tears started flowing. She expressed she was there as long as needed. I apologized to her and told her life was rough. I appreciated her genuineness in asking how I was doing. I told her it had been a while since anyone had asked, and it touched my heart. This act of kindness helped me over the hurdles of that day and encouraged me.

From out of left field, a childhood softball acquaintance invited me to golf. I immediately accepted as I was no longer included in Brennan's golf group. This invitation and nudge to get back on the golf course was like a medicine for my soul. I met another female golfer, and we three built a camaraderie. "The girls" weren't afraid of the heat and loved the game as much as I did. The invitation motivated me to start playing at my previous golf club. Returning to the golf course where I learned the game felt like coming home to family. Staff and members were warm and welcoming; it was a balm for my soul.

My daughter-in-law and her parents were friends. My daughter-in-law and her parents invited me to be a part of their holidays. I was so blessed and touched by their invitation and hospitality. They had no idea how they ministered to my heart by including me in their family holidays.

Friends Came from the Workplace

Co-workers I've worked with years ago to recently appeared with hearts of gold. They reached out early on and at various times. They never asked questions, only expressed sincere compassion. They sent encouraging text messages that always brought me to tears. A few invited me to have lunch. I was so happy to receive the invites. One blessed me with a meaningful gift. Each act was a hand on my mat and always perfect timing.

My current manager, Britni, and director, Aleisha, were friends. They both are wise and shared wisdom and insight, grounding me in truth. They checked in with me frequently, offering support. Britni is understanding and made me feel my well-being mattered to her. Aleisha and her husband helped me move furniture. They rented a U-Haul and helped me move to my second location, which was forty minutes away. I was deeply moved by their care and compassion. I am certain God placed me in that position with all this in mind.

Friends Came from the Church Body

In addition to the scripture in Mark, I want to share how important Hebrews 10:25 was to me. I share this because it goes hand in hand with the friend's reference in Mark. I've heard numerous people say their relationship with Jesus could be good without going to church. They would also say they don't have to go to church to be saved. I agreed; however, there is something sweeter in assembling with believers.

No judgment before I make this comment. I do not refer to people who are not able to attend church. This refers to those who are able but choose not to. My son is one example; yes, you, KZ. He says he has a relationship with God, and he doesn't have to go to church. I'm happy KZ is saved and has a relationship with God, no matter what it looks like. Just want to be clear: I don't feel anyone is less if they don't attend church because prayer and fellowship can occur anywhere. Pastor Zach Backues from Victory Life spoke about Life groups one Sunday. He said you can't practice Christianity alone, even though private communication with the Lord is great.

I hope you see through my story the significance in assembling with your brothers and sisters in Christ. I have a new appreciation for those who assembled during my storm. Those who were dedicated and served the members of the body. I was in desperate need of brothers and sisters in Christ to stand with me or carry my mat. They provided encouragement, edification, prayers, and declarations. I sought God's love and guidance through church members because it wasn't readily available outside of church. I attended church and a women's ministry regularly because I played a part in this. I had to request help, surrender, and obey.

The leader from the women's ministry I attended invited me for coffee. I didn't know her except seeing her at the monthly ministry and a quick hello. I accepted her invitation. She knew my husband from their previous church and inquired about his well-being. I only shared the skim of the surface information. She had no clue that week I was living out of my car and homeless. Most importantly, she had no idea of the impact of her invitation. I remember her gentle spirit; I felt she loved people. Her act of love touched me at one of the most embarrassing moments of my life, being homeless. I will never underestimate the power of a simple invitation.

At the women's ministry, I met a few ladies (the assembling of believers). They unknowingly placed a hand on my mat, carrying me closer to Jesus. I met one woman after I volunteered to help in the media words on the screen. Her presence was one of acceptance and love. She uplifted me each time I saw her at the ministry. She checked in on me, sent encouraging information, and prayed for me continually.

I met another woman at the women's ministry (assembling of believers). A lady approached me towards the end of the service. She explained she felt like she needed to come over and give me a hug as I wept alone and quietly. I started crying when she hugged me, not even aware of how much I needed human compassion. Her name is Tanya; we met for lunch one day. We had different stories but relatable suffering. It was nice to talk to someone who identified with what I was feeling. She understood me and listened, and it was good medicine when we visited. Tanya continues to reach out every now and then with a text or call. It's always at the right time.

RADIO AND TV CHURCH FRIENDS

I listened to various messages and felt they were a source of knowledge, encouragement, and motivation. Even though they were not physically present, they are considered a friend in Jesus. I know one day I will meet each one and thank them for their faithfulness in preaching the gospel. I hope they understand the impact they made on those who listened to their messages, even years after they were preached. The late Adrian Rogers has been a favorite for over a decade. I listen to his messages on the Love Worth Finding app daily when I commute. Andrew Wommack's Gospel Truth show was the first time I heard him and was changed drastically. I was so impressed I started Andrew Wommack's Charis Bible College. I also read and listen to Bill Johnson from Bethel Church in Redding, California. Each time I hear him speak, it moves me to a higher level of understanding. Bill Johnson's messages caused me to think from a different perspective, and I liked that about his messages. It wasn't until my chaos started that I stumbled upon Steven Furtick, and now I listen to him routinely. Steven Furtick had a way of moving me with his message, but I was physically moved when I listened to him. Steven

Furtick has a bold and courageous delivery. As he shared God's word, it strengthened me and caused me to take courage. Steven's messages were so encouraging I went back at least a year to hear more. Steven's messages always pulled me from the pit of sorrow and had a way of causing me to feel like I needed to get it together.

My Church Family—Victory Life

I was asked not to attend godly counsel by my husband. Therefore, the role of those who served in my church became a lifeline. After each church service, I approached a member of the ministry team. I'd share a broad-term description of what I needed prayer for. They filled me with God's love and encouragement. It was just in time and just what I needed.

I met a member of the prayer ministry at church; her name is Cindy Northcutt. She was usually stationed towards the back of the sanctuary. Cindy added me to her small group prayer list, and I felt she desired to see me through this. Anytime she and I see one another, we hug, and she prays over me. The prayer ministers were so important to me. Each one refueled me and renewed my hope and strength. Cindy continually placed a hand on my mat, carrying me a little closer to Jesus.

Another member of my church is a beautiful lady named Bridgett Hall. She became a family member from my first marriage. Bridgett continued to treat me like I was family after my first marriage ended. She was a steadfast friend and strong support throughout my chaos. Bridgett probably noticed something wasn't right before I even realized. I reached out to Bridgett when Brennan told me to get out. I was reluctant to reach out to her, but Brennan wanted me to move, or I thought he did at the time. After the fourth or fifth time, I discovered he really didn't mean it. I reached out to Bridgett because she and her husband own housing and apartments. She knew I was newly married, and she knew of my husband. I had to explain a little about what was going on, but I never felt judged. Bridgett checked for vacancies, letting me know they had something ready. Generally, Brennan and I would resolve our conflict in a few days, and I discovered I wouldn't be moving out. Bridgett followed up, and I explained we had worked through our issues and that I didn't need the housing. Bridgett reached out to me off and on from that point going forward. She continually prayed for me when we were having difficulties. She provided spiritual insight and guidance. Bridgett understood my battle wasn't flesh and blood and stood with me in prayer. I appreciated the love she extended to me. It meant a lot, and I felt like she was someone I could rely on for support. Bridgett's hand was on my mat continually as she remained steadfast.

Another member of my church, the one I referred to as The Wise Man-God's Truth Bearer, is Pastor Terry Brown. He holds a Doctorate in Ministry in Christian Counseling. He is well-versed in God's word, and I felt he was extremely beneficial to me. Four months post-relocation, I made an appointment with Pastor Terry because I was at my lowest. The first available appointment with Pastor Terry was a month out. During the month-long wait, I almost canceled the appointment. I experienced a shift in my well-being; I was improving. I kept the appointment and summarized the events over the last two to three months. After I finished speaking, what Pastor Terry shared next floored me. He said on January 2 (at my lowest), the Lord put me on his heart and said to pray for Ashley. Pastor Terry told me he asked the Lord what he needed to pray, and all he heard was just pray. Pastor Terry said he heard Ashley is on a roller coaster; she's going up and down vigorously, and she needs to get steady. Pastor Terry said he prayed (interceded), and I sat that day with a good report. I was awestruck at what he shared. I told Pastor Terry I wanted to go home and look at my journal entries. I wanted to see when the shift began because I had a drastic change for the better. I went home that evening and looked at my journal and found this written on January 4.

A Prayer for Help in Time of Trouble

Lord, don't be angry and rebuke me! Don't punish me in Your anger! I am worn out, O Lord; have pity on me! Give me strength; I am completely exhausted, and my whole being is deeply troubled. How long, O Lord, will You wait to help me? Come and save me, Lord; in Your mercy, rescue me from death. In the world of the dead, You are not remembered; no one can praise You there. I am worn out with grief. Every night, my bed is damp from my weeping, and my pillow is soaked with tears. I can hardly see; my eyes are so swollen from the weeping caused by my enemies. Keep away from me, you evil people! The Lord hears my weeping. He listens to my cry for help and will answer in prayer. My enemies will know the bitter shame of defeat; in sudden confusion, they will be driven away.

(Psalm 6:1–10)

Then, a few weeks after I prayed for help in time of trouble, I wrote (still unaware Pastor Terry interceded) in my journal: "I feel heartbrokenness decrease in intensity. I feel my thoughts of hurt, pain, loss, grief, and loneliness starting to dissipate. The fog is clearing. I feel alert, motivated, and encouraged. Thank You."

That exact day, I discovered, after hearing from Pastor Terry, the importance of praying for those who are on your heart!

Shortly after meeting with Pastor Terry, Pastor Zach spoke following praise and worship. I felt like Pastor Zach was the locker room coach who pumped up the players before the game. I felt myself being built up in spirit, encouraged, and ready for battle when he spoke. I received another image as he spoke about the woman in the Bible with the blood issue. In the vision, I saw myself as the woman with the issue. I had the understanding to be as courageous and intentional as her with my issues. I was on a mission carrying a boldness I'd never understood or considered. I was covered in courage, and I had a desire for Jesus, even the hem. I felt like his words empowered me.

I went to Pastor Zach and Serena, his spouse, after service to share the experience. They prayed over me, but neither knew about my situation. However, the words he spoke were directly related to my situation. Pastor Zach mentioned angelic presence, shackles being removed, gift of discernment, traumatic experiences being healed, dreams and visions, sound mind, and fog clearing. The fact that Pastor Zach said "fog clearing," and I wrote that in my journal, astounded me! Serena mentioned the image of a laundry basket and the significance in completing each task. I received two tasks from the Lord, and her word of knowledge was spot on.

Angelic presence has been mentioned to me a few times during the traumatic events. I saw the vision of the angel, and I believe I was continually surrounded by angels. I heard a message that angels wait for assignments; let us not forget to activate the angel assignments. Thank You, God, for assigning angels to watch over me and my family.

JESUS IS A FRIEND

Multiple times in this testimony, I stated I was alone, and that is not the truth. Physically, I was alone, but the most important friend never left my side. Jesus calls me friend; I was reminded of this by Pastor Zach and Serena when they referenced John 15:15 (NIV): "I no longer call you servants, because a servant does not know his master's business. Instead, I have called you friends, for everything that I learned from my Father I have made known to you." Knowing this truth and then proclaiming I'm alone instills conviction now. I knew Jesus was with me during the suffering. I could only explain the complete peace and comfort during the scariest of times as the love of Jesus. I felt His presence and protection surround me as I leaned into him and surrendered. He can and will meet your needs; you only need to ask.

"A man that hath friends must shew himself friendly: and there is a friend that sticketh closer than a brother".

(Proverbs 18:24, KJV)

For as long as I can remember, I've heard the saying, "It takes a village to raise a child." When I became a mother, I understood this saying a little more. I only related this saying to parents with young children. Life gets hectic, and what a blessing it is to have a village. A village of family and friends working together in unity and harmony for a common goal.

During my suffering, this saying crossed my path. I began reflecting on my life, from infancy to the current day. I saw the village step up in numerous acts of kindness and love. The same village from my early years was still present in adulthood. Now, I wondered if this saying should be restructured to include the young and old. Then I remembered this verse:

Behold what manner of love the Father has bestowed on us, that we should be called the children of God!

1 John 3:1a (NKJV)

No matter our age, we are all God's children. So that answered my own question about the saying.

The Fisherman

The fisherman experienced suffering due to an accident. Suffering may be self-inflicted, caused by another, or an accident. As I reflected on the fisherman story, I would say my situation was caused by another's actions and my choices. Another person's actions knocked me down and caused my initial injury. I made choices, thereafter impacting my future and well-being.

I had choices, much like the fisherman. Once I fell, I chose to stay on the ground. Distracting myself with the questions surrounding the fall (who, why, what). Day after day, caressing my injuries (loss, pain, heartache, despair, shame). I felt validated in staying knocked down. I deemed it acceptable to focus on the issues because someone did this to me. I felt I had a right to continually sob and be sad at the injustices of the traumatic situation.

I was unaware of how much damage was occurring the longer I lay on the ground. Refusing to seek help was destroying me. I wished someone would have asked me, "Ashley, what will the cost be? Ashley, your tab is growing for failing to seek help or making sensible choices." The unseen damage further complicated my situation, limiting my options. I was completely unaware of my condition or how to navigate through the complexities. I only saw the complications, wondering how I would ever get back to normalcy.

The fisherman sought medical care, and I sought God's help. I surrendered to Him and placed complete trust in Him with my life. I was slow to get off the ground. I gazed at and coddled my wounds longer than I should have. No matter what I did, I eventually got up and stood amidst the storm. I called upon my Father in heaven for help.

Chapter 16

———— ∞ ————

The Lesson

Once surrendered to God, I stumbled upon this scripture. I hear the Lord saying, "I will stay close to you, instructing you and guiding you along the pathway for your life. I will advise you along the way and lead you forth with my eyes as your guide!" (Psalm 32:8)

I didn't know what His help was going to look like, but I knew He would answer. I knew he had and never would leave me or forsake me, so I waited patiently. I had to purpose not to try to understand, only to trust where he would guide me. I still had pity parties, paralyzing fear, and numbness. As I remembered His promises or how good He's been, they began to diminish.

KZ is a fireman, and one day, he explained a rescue firemen utilize. I thought it fit my rescue perfectly. Television has warped our minds and deposited unrealistic expectations. I was fooled by this one, so I am guilty. The fireman rescue on television appears quick, easy, and effortless. The fireman enters the burning building, runs straight to the victims, and carries them out. I love that kind of rescue; I'm sure that happens too. I hoped my rescue would be quick and easy, but it wasn't.

My rescue was not the TV kind and was like the one KZ described. Bear with me as I attempt to describe it. The rescue I experienced was more like the one referred to as a primary search. I was deep in the darkness, and rescue was going to take some time. This type of search and rescue is utilized because the building is smoke-filled. The rescue is conducted by feel because the environment is pitch black. In these settings, there are multiple rooms, and the whereabouts and number of victims may be unknown. This rescue may start as a left or right wall search. A fireman and a partner enter a building. One teammate continually leaves a hand on the wall. The other teammate has twenty feet of webbing, allowing him to sweep the room for victims. The team scales the wall and rooms, searching for victims. The building is smoke-filled and hot, and vision completely obscured. If the fireman loses the wall contact, even for a second, they could become disoriented, becoming victims.

The firemen must use the same wall, tracing back on the same path out to safety. The victim, if able, must resist the urge to take over. Even when the escape route seems obvious. The victim and rescue team can't be deceived by the pockets of light they see on the way out. The pockets of light could be fire, a hole in the floor, or a hole in the wall, leading to danger. The victim must trust the fireman, as they have been trained for these situations. They know the best practice rescue strategies, and it's vital the victims wait patiently. The fireman understands this saying all too well, "Slow is steady, and steady is fast." I say all this to express the importance of trust and patience in our Rescuer. The Lord reminds us His ways and thoughts are higher than ours (Isaiah 55:8–9). Don't lose heart when your rescue hasn't taken place like you envisioned or in your time.

And call upon me in the day of trouble:
I will deliver thee, and thou shalt glorify me.

Psalm 50:15 (KJV)

CAUGHT OFF GUARD

One of the hardest things to get over was a broken heart. Everything in life reminded me of my husband and our marriage. I was constantly reminded of what it was when I saw a movie, a smell, a couple holding hands, a football game, a flower, a town, TV shows, and foods. Many inconspicuous things served as constant reminders of what I no longer had.

I heard something that caused me to think differently in a message from Bill Johnson, Healing a Broken Heart. "When He brings healing to a broken heart, He doesn't start with answers. We engage in surrender." Bill Johnson went on to say that remaining unwilling to come to the Lord for healing will result in hardness of heart.

I was driving home one day while I was writing this portion of my testimony. I talked to God about not getting explanations in suffering. I voiced to God I understood we don't always get answers and aren't owed any. I expressed to Him it would be nice to have some insight in the brokenness and why we couldn't work this out. I knew Brennan loved me immensely at one time. I felt he loved me now, but it wasn't the same. I had a superb ability to work with difficult people and conflict resolution from years of experience. I couldn't get anywhere with Brennan, and I didn't understand.

Shortly after, I received a visual picture of my love and Brennan's love. In my wedding vows, I said I wanted to show Brennan God's kind of love, and the Lord revealed this image. Love was demonstrated as water in the image, and Brennan had a well full of water (love). I saw every time we disagreed or I disappointed or hurt him. Brennan drew out the measure of water in relation to the amount of hurt, pain, or disappointment he felt. The Lord showed me that Brennan had drawn out almost all the water (love for me), and only ounces remained. I realized Brennan didn't have the capacity to extend love because it was no longer there.

The Lord then revealed a different image of what my love for Brennan looked like. My love was like a natural spring with a never-ending supply. No amount of water drawn out affected the love I have for my husband. No matter how egregious or deliberate the acts towards me were, it didn't change my love. I knew this was the kind of love Jesus has for us, except it's not a spring; it's much bigger. The Lord revealed our love for one another was not the same. My husband's love is conditional, and my love is unconditional. I instantly recalled what he told me about my son's table manners. Brennan said he couldn't blame my son for his lack of table manners because "he wasn't taught any better." I realized I couldn't blame Brennan for his type of love for the same reason.

I feel sickened when I think about the time I put forth and tears I cried for a human man. I hadn't shed one tear for Jesus. That's very shameful when you think about it. Jesus was gruesomely beaten, crucified, sacrificed himself, and died for me and you. Jesus knew I hadn't shed a tear for Him, yet he still loved me and rescued me. Nothing changed on His end. Isn't that amazing?

FROM STEVEN FURTICK'S MESSAGE "NEVER STOP KNOCKING"

Freedom comes through obedience. Have you ever been delivered from something in your life, but at one time, you thought, *I'll never be free of this?* And now, by the grace of God, you are free. You didn't get free by thinking about it. You got free by taking action. You reached out to somebody. You prayed, you went to God with it, and He answered. You knocked, but you also did more than that: you obeyed.

Adrian Rogers said, in great loss, there is great treasure. Mr. Rogers shared this verse:

Blessed be the God and Father of our Lord Jesus Christ, the Father of compassion and the God of all comfort, who comforts us in all our troubles, so that we can comfort those in any trouble with the comfort we ourselves have received from God.

2 Corinthians 1:3–4 (NIV)

Mr. Rogers explained there is something about a person who bears the scars and has that testimony that no one else has. I bear unique scars now that will present opportunities to comfort others. The wounds were painful and deep; however, they would heal through God's grace and become scars.

I leave you with this story and hope it serves as a reminder in your future needs.

I was about sixteen years old, working an evening shift after school at a popular fast-food restaurant. The drive-thru slowed down, allowing me to tend to the tasks that were hard to get to when it was busy. I restocked cups, lids, condiments, and Happy Meal boxes and cleaned my area. While I was cleaning, I noticed a device I had never seen before under the register. I looked at it thoroughly and thought it resembled a garage door opener and began to wonder what it operated. I found no identifying information, so I pressed the single button on the front and waited for something to happen. I scanned all the screens and gadgets, and nothing was visibly changing. I looked at the workers around me to see if they noticed anything happening. They continued in their normal activities; I assumed they witnessed no changes. I listened very carefully and heard nothing out of the ordinary. I continued to search for something to change, and nothing happened. I finally concluded it was a lost item. Figuring a worker placed it there in case someone was looking for it, so I put it back where I found it.

I went back to cleaning and restocking. As I walked towards the front counter, all of a sudden, lights and sirens surrounded the place within seconds. Men in uniforms rushed inside and asked with urgency what was going on. I was unaware of anything, shrugging my shoulders. The manager came to the front to greet the members of law enforcement. The manager also asked around, and no one knew. A member of the law enforcement team said, "Ma'am, someone hit the panic button." I immediately felt a heat wave rush through me, and embarrassment struck me. I grabbed the device I found a few moments ago and asked, "Is this the panic button?" The manager confirmed it was. I admitted it was me with a sheepish smile and apologized. The law enforcement team seemed relieved it was a false alarm and left immediately. The manager chuckled about it, and I apologized once more.

I bring this story up for one reason, and it relates to the panic button. I was awestruck at the power of a button in the drive-thru. I realized what was possible with a simple press of a button. I knew if danger presented in that restaurant, a rescue plan would be activated immediately at the touch of a button. I had faith in the reliability and certainty of the drive-through panic button.

I saw an image of our prayers in times of trouble as our own personal panic button. Our prayers (panic button) are sent directly and immediately to our Father in heaven. The very moment I prayed to my heavenly Father in times of trouble, He initiated a rescue plan. Just as I was unaware of the law enforcement rescue plan that day, I would not be able to see God's rescue plan being activated. I would not see heavenly actions being taken on my behalf. I would not hear God's whispers being disclosed to His disciples. Whispers containing well-timed acts of love, serving as reminders of His presence and steadfast love. We serve the God of angel armies, and I would not see Him give angels charge over me. I knew, with certainty, the police would rescue me if I activated the panic button at the restaurant. So,

CAUGHT OFF GUARD

how much more would our Father act on our behalf when we activate the panic button (prayer) to Him?

The very moment I call to you for a fathers help the tide of the battle turns and my enemies flee.

Psalm 56:9 (TPT)

Fisherman Transformed to a Fisher of Men

Now, the fisherman is a fisher of men. "When we fish for fish, we take them out of a beautiful life into death. But when we fish for men, we take them out of death into a beautiful life."[9]

---

9   Matthew 4:18–20, *The Adrian Rogers Legacy Bible*, 2009, by Love Worth Finding Ministries, Inc.

Epilogue

Twenty months after the day my life changed forever, I concluded my testimony. My story is not over yet. I will face additional challenges as civil matters are resolved. These include divorce, business lawsuits, and IRS matters. However, I am confident that God will see me through. I will use my experiences to help others who are struggling.

Afterword

I began writing my testimony a year after I relocated and over the course of five months. Unexpectedly, the process of writing became a way for me to process my own experiences. I was surprised to learn that writing was a part of my healing process.

I hope my testimony has resonated with you in some way. For those who are suffering, I pray that your faith in God will increase. If you are not experiencing difficulties, I hope that my testimony will inspire you to be more intentional in your daily encounters. I pray that we can all be more like the friends of the paralyzed man in Mark 2:1–5.

Printed in the USA
CPSIA information can be obtained
at www.ICGtesting.com
LVHW012020250124
769291LV00015B/686